George W. Bush

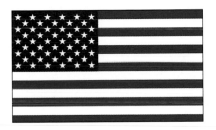

Veda Boyd Jones

CHELSEA HOUSE
PUBLISHERS
A Haights Cross Communications Company

Philadelphia

CHELSEA HOUSE PUBLISHERS

EDITOR IN CHIEF Sally Cheney
DIRECTOR OF PRODUCTION Kim Shinners
CREATIVE MANAGER Takeshi Takahashi
MANUFACTURING MANAGER Diann Grasse

Staff for GEORGE W. BUSH

EDITOR Lee Marcott
ASSOCIATE EDITOR Patrick Stone
PRODUCTION ASSISTANT Jaimie Winkler
PICTURE RESEARCH 21st Century Publishing and Communications, Inc.
SERIES DESIGNER Takeshi Takahashi
COVER DESIGNER Keith Trego
LAYOUT 21st Century Publishing and Communications, Inc.

A Haights Cross Communications ✦ Company

http://www.chelseahouse.com

3 5 7 9 8 6 4 2

Library of Congress Cataloging-in-Publication Data

Jones, Veda Boyd.
   George W. Bush / Veda Boyd Jones.
      p. cm. — (Major world leaders)
Includes index.
   ISBN 0-7910-6940-0 (hardcover) — ISBN 0-7910-7184-7 (pbk.)
   1. Bush, George W. (George Walker), 1946–   —Juvenile literature. 2. Presidents—
United States—Biography—Juvenile literature. I Title. II. Series.
E903 .J66 2002
973.931'092—dc21
                                                          2002009101

TABLE OF CONTENTS

On Leadership

Arthur M. Schlesinger, jr.

Leadership, it may be said, is really what makes the world go round. Love no doubt smoothes the passage; but love is a private transaction between consenting adults. Leadership is a public transaction with history. The idea of leadership affirms the capacity of individuals to move, inspire, and mobilize masses of people so that they act together in pursuit of an end. Sometimes leadership serves good purposes, sometimes bad; but whether the end is benign or evil, great leaders are those men and women who leave their personal stamp on history.

Now, the very concept of leadership implies the proposition that individuals can make a difference. This proposition has never been universally accepted. From classical times to the present day, eminent thinkers have regarded individuals as no more than the agents and pawns of larger forces, whether the gods and goddesses of the ancient world or, in the modern era, race, class, nation, the dialectic, the will of the people, the spirit of the times, history itself. Against such forces, the individual dwindles into insignificance.

So contends the thesis of historical determinism. Tolstoy's great novel *War and Peace* offers a famous statement of the case. Why, Tolstoy asked, did millions of men in the Napoleonic Wars, denying their human feelings and their common sense, move back and forth across Europe slaughtering their fellows? "The war," Tolstoy answered, "was bound to happen simply because it was bound to happen." All prior history determined it. As for leaders, they, Tolstoy said, "are but the labels that serve to give a name to an end and, like labels, they have the least possible connection with the event." The greater the leader, "the more conspicuous the inevitability and the predestination of every act he commits." The leader, said Tolstoy, is "the slave of history."

Determinism takes many forms. Marxism is the determinism of class. Nazism the determinism of race. But the idea of men and women as the slaves of history runs athwart the deepest human instincts. Rigid determinism abolishes the idea of human freedom—the assumption of free choice that underlies every move we make, every word we speak, every thought we think. It abolishes the idea of human responsibility, since it is manifestly unfair to reward or punish people for actions that are by definition beyond their control. No one can live consistently by any deterministic creed. The Marxist states prove this themselves by their extreme susceptibility to the cult of leadership.

More than that, history refutes the idea that individuals make no difference. In December 1931 a British politician crossing Fifth Avenue in New York City between 76th and 77th Streets around 10:30 P.M. looked in the wrong direction and was knocked down by an automobile—a moment, he later recalled, of a man aghast, a world aglare: "I do not understand why I was not broken like an eggshell or squashed like a gooseberry." Fourteen months later an American politician, sitting in an open car in Miami, Florida, was fired on by an assassin; the man beside him was hit. Those who believe that individuals make no difference to history might well ponder whether the next two decades would have been the same had Mario Constasino's car killed Winston Churchill in 1931 and Giuseppe Zangara's bullet killed Franklin Roosevelt in 1933. Suppose, in addition, that Lenin had died of typhus in Siberia in 1895 and that Hitler had been killed on the western front in 1916. What would the 20th century have looked like now?

For better or for worse, individuals do make a difference. "The notion that a people can run itself and its affairs anonymously," wrote the philosopher William James, "is now well known to be the silliest of absurdities. Mankind does nothing save through initiatives on the part of inventors, great or small, and imitation by the rest of us—these are the sole factors in human progress. Individuals of genius show the way, and set the patterns, which common people then adopt and follow."

Leadership, James suggests, means leadership in thought as well as in action. In the long run, leaders in thought may well make the greater difference to the world. "The ideas of economists and political philosophers, both when they are right and when they are wrong," wrote John Maynard Keynes, "are more powerful than is commonly understood. Indeed the world is ruled by little else. Practical men, who believe themselves to be quite exempt from any intellectual influences, are usually the slaves of some defunct economist. . . . The power of vested interests is vastly exaggerated compared with the gradual encroachment of ideas."

But, as Woodrow Wilson once said, "Those only are leaders of men, in the general eye, who lead in action. . . . It is at their hands that new thought gets its translation into the crude language of deeds." Leaders in thought often invent in solitude and obscurity, leaving to later generations the tasks of imitation. Leaders in action—the leaders portrayed in this series—have to be effective in their own time.

And they cannot be effective by themselves. They must act in response to the rhythms of their age. Their genius must be adapted, in a phrase from William James, "to the receptivities of the moment." Leaders are useless without followers. "There goes the mob," said the French politician, hearing a clamor in the streets. "I am their leader. I must follow them." Great leaders turn the inchoate emotions of the mob to purposes of their own. They seize on the opportunities of their time, the hopes, fears, frustrations, crises, potentialities. They succeed when events have prepared the way for them, when the community is awaiting to be aroused, when they can provide the clarifying and organizing ideas. Leadership completes the circuit between the individual and the mass and thereby alters history.

It may alter history for better or for worse. Leaders have been responsible for the most extravagant follies and most monstrous crimes that have beset suffering humanity. They have also been vital in such gains as humanity has made in individual freedom, religious and racial tolerance, social justice, and respect for human rights.

There is no sure way to tell in advance who is going to lead for good and who for evil. But a glance at the gallery of men and women in MAJOR WORLD LEADERS suggests some useful tests.

One test is this: Do leaders lead by force or by persuasion? By command or by consent? Through most of history leadership was exercised by the divine right of authority. The duty of followers was to defer and to obey. "Theirs not to reason why/Theirs but to do and die." On occasion, as with the so-called enlightened despots of the 18th century in Europe, absolutist leadership was animated by humane purposes. More often, absolutism nourished the passion for domination, land, gold, and conquest and resulted in tyranny.

The great revolution of modern times has been the revolution of equality. "Perhaps no form of government," wrote the British historian James Bryce in his study of the United States, *The American Commonwealth,* "needs great leaders so much as democracy." The idea that all people should be equal in their legal condition has undermined the old structure of authority, hierarchy, and deference. The revolution of equality has had two contrary effects on the nature of leadership. For equality, as Alexis de Tocqueville pointed out in his great study *Democracy in America*, might mean equality in servitude as well as equality in freedom.

"I know of only two methods of establishing equality in the political world," Tocqueville wrote. "Rights must be given to every citizen, or none at all to anyone . . . save one, who is the master of all." There was no middle ground "between the sovereignty of all and the absolute power of one man." In his astonishing prediction of 20th-century totalitarian dictatorship, Tocqueville explained how the revolution of equality could lead to the *Führerprinzip* and more terrible absolutism than the world had ever known.

But when rights are given to every citizen and the sovereignty of all is established, the problem of leadership takes a new form, becomes more exacting than ever before. It is easy to issue commands and enforce them by the rope and the stake, the concentration camp and the *gulag*. It is much harder to use argument and achievement to overcome opposition and win consent. The Founding Fathers of the United States understood the difficulty. They believed that history had given them the opportunity to decide, as Alexander Hamilton wrote in the first Federalist Paper, whether men are indeed capable of basing government on "reflection and choice, or whether they are forever destined to depend . . . on accident and force."

Government by reflection and choice called for a new style of leadership and a new quality of followership. It required leaders to be responsive to popular concerns, and it required followers to be active and informed participants in the process. Democracy does not eliminate emotion from politics; sometimes it fosters demagoguery; but it is confident that, as the greatest of democratic leaders put it, you cannot fool all of the people all of the time. It measures leadership by results and retires those who overreach or falter or fail.

It is true that in the long run despots are measured by results too. But they can postpone the day of judgment, sometimes indefinitely, and in the meantime they can do infinite harm. It is also true that democracy is no guarantee of virtue and intelligence in government, for the voice of the people is not necessarily the voice of God. But democracy, by assuring the right of opposition, offers built-in resistance to the evils inherent in absolutism. As the theologian Reinhold Niebuhr summed it up, "Man's capacity for justice makes democracy possible, but man's inclination to justice makes democracy necessary."

A second test for leadership is the end for which power is sought. When leaders have as their goal the supremacy of a master race or the promotion of totalitarian revolution or the acquisition and exploitation of colonies or the protection of greed and privilege or the preservation of personal power, it is likely that their leadership will do little to advance the cause of humanity. When their goal is the abolition of slavery, the liberation of women, the enlargement of opportunity for the poor and powerless, the extension of equal rights to racial minorities, the defense of the freedoms of expression and opposition, it is likely that their leadership will increase the sum of human liberty and welfare.

Leaders have done great harm to the world. They have also conferred great benefits. You will find both sorts in this series. Even "good" leaders must be regarded with a certain wariness. Leaders are not demigods; they put on their trousers one leg after another just like ordinary mortals. No leader is infallible, and every leader needs to be reminded of this at regular intervals. Irreverence irritates leaders but is their salvation. Unquestioning submission corrupts leaders and demeans followers. Making a cult of a leader is always a mistake. Fortunately hero worship generates its own antidote. "Every hero," said Emerson, "becomes a bore at last."

The signal benefit the great leaders confer is to embolden the rest of us to live according to our own best selves, to be active, insistent, and resolute in affirming our own sense of things. For great leaders attest to the reality of human freedom against the supposed inevitabilities of history. And they attest to the wisdom and power that may lie within the most unlikely of us, which is why Abraham Lincoln remains the supreme example of great leadership. A great leader, said Emerson, exhibits new possibilities to all humanity. "We feed on genius . . . . Great men exist that there may be greater men."

Great leaders, in short, justify themselves by emancipating and empowering their followers. So humanity struggles to master its destiny, remembering with Alexis de Tocqueville: "It is true that around every man a fatal circle is traced beyond which he cannot pass; but within the wide verge of that circle he is powerful and free; as it is with man, so with communities." ▪

A hijacked commercial plane approaches the World Trade Center shortly before crashing into the landmark skyscraper, September 11, 2001.

1

Attack on the Nation

President George W. Bush awoke before daylight on September 11, 2001, and slipped into khaki shorts, a large white tee shirt, socks and running shoes; he was off for a jog. Never mind that he wasn't at home in Washington, D.C. Even on the road, like this day in Sarasota, Florida, he wanted to get the kinks out, release energy, and start his day right.

Reporters followed the president on his run, and by the time he was walking in his cool-down phase, the sun had peeked over the horizon. A reporter asked how many miles he'd run, and the president replied, "Four and a half."

Bush returned to his hotel, received his routine national security briefing, and arrived at Emma E. Booker Elementary School eager to speak about reading and education. Before he was introduced to a class of second graders, he was taken to a holding room and informed that a plane had hit the north tower of the World Trade Center in New York City. A myriad of possibilities raced through his mind. Surely it had been an accident, a plane with mechanical failure, a pilot trying to ditch the plane in the harbor and missing.

Bush, with a pensive countenance, left the holding room and was introduced to the second graders. He was listening to them read when chief-of-staff Andrew Card walked into the room and whispered in the president's right ear that another plane had flown into the second tower. The president's head reeled to the left, as if he'd been hit. He bit his lip, and his gaze darted from the students to the floor to the teacher, his distracted thoughts not on reading, but on what had to be a terrorist attack on the United States. For six long minutes he sat in the classroom so he wouldn't alarm the children. As he rose to his feet to walk out, a reporter asked him if he was aware that a plane had crashed in New York.

He held up his hand as if to stop the words. "We'll talk about it later," he said and strode to the holding room where he was updated on the horrific events. He immediately placed phone calls while watching TV pictures of the two burning towers.

Around 9:30, over a half-hour late for his scheduled speech, he was ushered into a large room where 200 local officials, school administrators, teachers, and students waited. Instead of his prepared speech, a solemn president explained that others would be discussing education in his place and he would be returning to Washington. In a stiff manner he read:

> Today we've had a national tragedy. Two airplanes have crashed into the World Trade Center in an apparent terrorist attack on our country.
>
> I have spoken to the Vice President, to the Governor of New York, to the Director of the FBI, and have ordered that the full resources of the federal government go to help the victims and their families, and to conduct a full-scale investigation to hunt down and to find those folks who committed this act.
>
> Terrorism against our nation will not stand.

President George W. Bush speaks to Vice President Dick Cheney by telephone aboard Air Force One after departing Offutt Air Force Base in Nebraska, September 11.

As President Bush was taken to the Sarasota airport, where bomb-sniffing dogs had thoroughly searched Air Force One, he learned that the terrorist attack wasn't over. Another hijacked plane had hit the west side of the Pentagon. Within minutes, the White House was evacuated after authorities determined it could be the destination of a fourth hijacked plane.

Forced by Federal Bureau of Investigation agents to a bombproof shelter in the basement of the White House, Vice President Dick Cheney picked up a secure phone and called the president. He strongly urged him to delay his return. FBI and other law enforcement agencies believed that not only the White House, but also the president's plane was a target.

Air Force One took off from Florida with a secret destination and with a fighter escort. It flew at a high altitude and changed directions several times. In his office in the plane, Bush watched on TV as the twin towers collapsed and spoke on the phone to his wife and to his advisors. He was overheard saying, "That's what we're paid for, boys. We're gonna take care of this. We're going to find out who did this. They're not going to like me as President."

Already the Federal Aviation Agency had shut down all U.S. airports, and air traffic controllers were scrambling to land all airborne planes at the nearest airports. Bush had made the decision for the military to shoot down any other hijacked planes if they approached populated areas. Bridges into Manhattan were closed. Wall Street had halted trading. Warships were taking up positions off the East Coast. Across America, citizens were watching TV in shock, numb with disbelief.

Bush wanted to speak to the nation before his plane reached its ultimate destination, Offutt Air Force Base in Nebraska, the most secure military post in the country. By now the president knew that a fourth hijacked plane had crashed in a Pennsylvania field instead of its planned target, which FBI surmised to be the White House or the Capitol.

Bush's plane scheduled a stop at Barksdale Air Force Base near Shreveport, Louisiana. Two fighter jets, one on each wing, escorted the plane to the airstrip. Only when local reporters discovered that Air Force One had landed did the rest of the country know the whereabouts of the president.

Bush was ushered by military guards in full combat gear to a building where he delivered a message to TV cameras. "Freedom itself was attacked this morning by a faceless coward. And freedom will be defended . . . The United States will hunt down and punish those responsible for these cowardly acts." Reading from a script, a stern-faced Bush informed Americans that U.S. military at home and abroad was on high alert status and that security precautions were in place to insure the functions of the government. "The resolve of our great nation is being tested. But make no mistake: We will show the world that we will pass this test."

Once again, Bush climbed the steps to board Air Force One, and this time he was flown to Nebraska. Here he was secured in an underground bunker where he held a teleconference with the National Security Council. Together they pieced together options and mapped out strategies for dealing with the changes forced on American life.

Meanwhile at FBI headquarters in Washington, Bush's trusted counselor Karen Hughes spoke to the press, assuring Americans that the president had directed that the federal emergency response plan be implemented. Secret Service had secured members of the national security team, the Cabinet, and senior staff members in various locations. The government was operating. Banks were open. Health and Human Services had sent personnel and supplies to the attack scenes.

Around 4:30 P.M., President Bush headed back to his

airplane, telling reporters he wasn't going to let some tinhorn terrorist keep him out of Washington. He arrived in Washington around 7:00 P.M. and addressed the nation from the Oval Office at 8:30. He talked about the victims of the attack.

> These acts of mass murder were intended to frighten our nation into chaos and retreat. But they have failed; our country is strong.
>
> A great people has been moved to defend a great nation. Terrorist attacks can shake the foundations of our biggest buildings, but they cannot touch the foundation of America. These acts shattered steel, but they cannot dent the steel of American resolve.
>
> America was targeted for attack because we're the brightest beacon for freedom and opportunity in the world. And no one will keep that light from shining.

President Bush assured the nation that the evacuations of government buildings on this day were for security reasons, but they would be open for business the next day. He thanked world leaders who had called with condolences and offers of help. In one sentence he summed up how he was going to find the terrorists. "We will make no distinction between the terrorists who committed these acts and those who harbor them."

On Wednesday, the 12th, the nation was still in shock. Bush pushed the rhetoric up a notch, saying the attacks were more than acts of terror—they were acts of war.

Bush was criticized by some for not being in the public eye for six long hours while he was in the secure bunker in Nebraska. Government spokesmen again reiterated that Air Force One was a suspected target. Indeed, on Wednesday morning an airplane, which on Tuesday had taken off from New Jersey and flown its routine route to Florida, was

President Bush is seen through the windows of the Oval Office of the White House in Washington, September 11, as he addresses the nation about the terrorist attacks on the World Trade Center and the Pentagon.

swarming with FBI agents, who suspected this plane would have been a fifth hijacked plane had terrorists' plans not somehow gone awry.

Late afternoon on Wednesday, Bush and Secretary of Defense Donald Rumsfeld visited the Pentagon. Bush addressed the workers and said he felt both sad and angry, but his remarks seemed scripted.

Thursday morning Bush paced behind his desk in the Oval Office while talking on the phone to New York City Mayor Rudy Giuliani and New York Governor George Pataki. It was a photo opportunity with cameras on the two men in New York and on the president in Washington. Bush's words were awkward and sounded unnatural; a replay of words spoken earlier about a new kind of war. His words sounded like a poorly rehearsed speech.

After he hung up the phone, he took a few questions from reporters. He justified not returning immediately to Washington as an appropriate action for a commander-in-chief and then took a question about his prayers during this time. He said he was thinking about the victims. Fighting back tears, he said, "I am a loving guy, and I am also someone, however, who has got a job to do, and I intend to do it. This country will not relent until we have saved ourselves and others from the terrible tragedy that came upon America." This was the leader Americans had been waiting to see— a man shaken by emotions, but resolved to make good decisions that would see the country through the disaster and the days of his promised war against terrorism.

When Bush met with the two senators from New York, Hillary Rodham Clinton and Charles Schumer, offering aid for their state, they asked for $20 billion. He didn't hesitate, but immediately agreed that it was appropriate help for New York City. He also commented on the cost of the war that he knew would take time to plan.

"When I take action, I'm not going to fire a $2 million missile at a $10 empty tent and hit a camel in the butt. It's going to be decisive."

On Friday, President Bush spoke at the Washington National Cathedral at the National Day of Prayer and Remembrance for those lost in the attacks. Seated beside him and First Lady Laura Bush were his parents, former president George H.W. Bush and Barbara Bush. Former presidents Bill Clinton, Jimmy Carter, and Gerald Ford and their wives sat in the congregation. Bush had also invited former vice president Al Gore, whom he had defeated for the high office less than a year earlier in a tight and highly contested election. Solidarity was in the faces of these officials; they were all Americans first and partisan politicians second as they listened to Bush's eloquent words.

> War has been waged against us by stealth and deceit and murder. This nation is peaceful, but fierce when stirred to anger. This conflict was begun on the timing and terms of others. It will end in a way, and at an hour, of our choosing.
>
> In every generation, the world has produced enemies of human freedom. They have attacked America, because we are freedom's home and defender. And the commitment of our fathers is now the calling of our time.

When President Bush took his seat, his father reached out and patted his arm in a gesture of respect and approval, a gesture that reflected the feelings of a nation. The younger man shook his father's hand.

That afternoon President Bush flew to New York City and was stunned by the sight at "Ground Zero," the site where the Twin Towers had stood. Smoke still rose from the many fires in the debris as he walked among the ruins.

Someone handed him a bullhorn. In a loud voice he told somber rescue workers that the nation mourned with them. Someone yelled, "I can't hear you." He yelled back, "I can hear you." The crowd erupted in cheers and laughter, a first since that awful Tuesday. The president repeated, "I can hear you. The rest of the world hears you." Again he was interrupted with applause. "And the people who knocked these buildings down will hear all of us soon." The crowd chanted, "U.S.A! U.S.A!" The president had connected with

As rescue efforts continue in the rubble of the World Trade Center, President Bush greets firefighters at the site during a tour of the devastation, September 14. After viewing the site from a helicopter, Bush toured the area on foot.

the workers and rallied them when they were in great need of an emotional lift.

That night in Washington, Congress granted Bush the power to make war, and the plans to wage the war against terrorism continued to take shape in meetings at the Pentagon and meetings with the National Security Council. Bush told Americans that this war would not be like other wars, and he identified as a prime suspect Osama bin Laden, who organized terrorist training camps in Afghanistan and whose work had been supported by the Taliban regime, the rulers of that country. The terrain of that desolate land would demand a different type of warfare.

Bush also reminded Americans that it was time to go back to work, to get the country moving forward, and to fight terrorism by not letting it intimidate America. To underscore this message, on Monday, the 17th, he went to the Executive Office Building next to the White House and met office workers as they arrived for work.

That afternoon he spoke briefly at the Islamic Center in Washington. Because the terrorists had been identified with the extremist Muslim terrorist group al-Qaeda, across the nation there had been isolated negative reactions against Arabs and followers of the Islamic religion. Bush's remarks were aimed at making a distinction between the terrorists and Muslims. "The face of terror is not the true faith of Islam. Islam is peace," he said.

Bush needed a bigger pulpit to deliver his message that the war wasn't against Arabs but against a specific segment, and that pulpit was at the Capitol in front of a joint session of Congress.

On September 20th, Bush strode into the great hall and gave the speech of his life. Some 82 million Americans watched on television, and Bush held the attention of millions more around the world. Newspapers printed the full text of his eloquent message the next day.

President Bush is applauded on Capitol Hill on September 20, 2001, during his address before a joint session of Congress.

In his speech, Bush demanded that the Taliban turn over bin Laden or they would share in the fate of that terrorist. He spoke to nations around the world, saying they had a decision to make: either they were with the United States or they were with the terrorists. And he told Americans:

> Great harm has been done to us. We have suffered great loss. And in our grief and anger we have found our mission and our moment. Freedom and fear are at war. The advance of human freedom—the great achievement of our time, and the great hope of every time—now depends on us. Our nation—this generation—will lift a dark threat of violence from our people and our future. We will rally the world to this cause by our efforts, by our courage. We will not tire, we will not falter, and we will not fail.

The leader of this generation was facing the challenge. George W. Bush had found his mission and his moment.

George W. Bush on his father's shoulders on the Yale University campus, New Haven, Connecticut, ca. 1947.

2

Growing Up in Texas

George Walker Bush was born on July 6, 1946, in New Haven, Connecticut, to a family heritage of success in business, high social status, and public service. He had a tradition to live up to, and he inherited some of the abilities that would allow him to do just that from several charismatic ancestors.

His great-grandfather, Samuel P. Bush, amassed a fortune through the railroad and steel industries, which started the family empire. As a businessman, he was well respected and was a charter member of the United States Chamber of Commerce. He also served as a key advisor to President Herbert Hoover, which began the family's association with high-powered political figures.

George W.'s grandfather, Prescott Bush, continued the family traditions and added success in sports to a long list of achievements. He played both baseball and football for Yale University, enjoyed golf, and much later shot a record golf round in the U.S. Seniors Championship. Prescott Bush married Dorothy Walker, whose father co-founded Brown Brothers Harriman, the oldest private investment firm on Wall Street. The Walker family had several family homes, and among them was Walker's Point in Kennebunkport, Maine, which would be a place where George W. would play with his cousins and enjoy the close family ties of the Bush-Walker clan.

Prescott Bush served his country as a soldier in World War I and later as a U.S. senator from Connecticut. He liked order and preciseness, whether at his office at his father-in-law's stockbroker firm in New York City, at his home in Greenwich, Connecticut, or at his vacation retreat in Kennebunkport. He demanded that his children be well-behaved and mannerly around him. His wife expected the children to be aggressive in sports and give their best to every activity in which they were involved.

With two strong-willed parents, George W.'s father, George Herbert Walker Bush, grew up in a home full of expectations, competitiveness, exquisite manners, and lots of love for family and extended family. George Bush attended a private prep school where he excelled both academically and athletically, and although he'd been accepted at Yale University, he decided to step directly from high school graduation exercises into the military. At the age of 18, he became the youngest pilot in the U.S. Navy at that time, and at age 20, in 1944, his plane was shot down in World War II's Pacific theater. He survived in a life raft until a submarine rescued him, and two months later he returned to his ship. When his squadron returned home, he married Barbara Pierce and spent the remainder of his military service at various bases in the United States.

Barbara Pierce Bush, George W.'s mother, was the daughter of the president of McCall Publishing Company. She met George Bush at a dance when she was just 16 and was immediately attracted to him. They became secretly engaged the summer before he shipped out and before she started her freshman year at Smith College. She dropped out of college during her sophomore year when she married him. Once he was out of the service in 1945, they moved to New Haven, Connecticut, and George Bush enrolled at Yale in a special two-and-a-half-year degree program. The G.I. Bill paid his tuition, and his savings from his Navy years paid the rent. Although his family was wealthy and willing to invest in worthwhile projects of family members, they felt a married son should stand on his own two feet.

When George W. Bush was born, his father was a sophomore at Yale. As new parents, Barbara and George mimicked the parenting style of their parents. Barbara's father had told her "the three most important things you can give your children are: the best education, a good example, and all the love in the world." She and George set out to follow that advice.

As the elder George attended classes, studied, and played on the Yale baseball team, Barbara took care of the baby in their small apartment where they shared a kitchen with two other families. She took little George to baseball games to watch his father play first base.

During George Bush's final year at Yale, he interviewed with several firms. His degree in economics would have helped him in a number of jobs, and he could easily have headed to Wall Street and followed in his father's footsteps. However, he wanted to work with something tangible, not intangible numbers, and he and Barbara both wanted to make a life of their own, away from their parents' expectations. He accepted a job with an old family friend at Dresser Industries, a holding company that had several oil-related subsidiaries, including one that made equipment for oil and gas businesses.

George Bush loaded his brand new red Studebaker, a graduation present from his parents, and headed for Odessa,

Texas, a town where mostly blue-collar workers, like Bush, lived and worked. His job was manual labor—painting oilrigs, sweeping the floor of the shop, working on slippery rig clutches—but he gladly started at the bottom of the oil business to learn every element of it.

After George found a place for his family to live, Barbara and little George flew to Texas. Their duplex apartment consisted of two rooms; the Bushes shared a bathroom with occupants of the other apartment. By Christmas the family had moved to another apartment, but because George W.'s father only had Sundays and one Saturday afternoon every three weeks off work, they couldn't make it back East for Christmas with the family. It was time to create their own traditions in their adopted state.

West Texas, where every tree and flower had to be carefully cultivated, had nothing in common with lush green Connecticut, but George W. loved the flat, dry, sandy place, which was his first memory of home. His father wrote to a friend about the two-year-old: "Whenever I come home he greets me and talks a blue streak, sentences disjointed of course but enthusiasm and spirit boundless. . . . The great thing is that he seems to be very happy wherever he is and he is very good about amusing himself in the small yard we have here."

Barbara Bush was also making the best of a different situation. As she wrote in her memoirs, she learned early that "You have two choices in life. You can like what you do, or you can dislike it. I have chosen to like it." Her positive attitude rubbed off on her son.

The Bushes were in Odessa for less than a year when George Bush was transferred to California. There the family moved around, living in motels and rented places, as George worked eight-hour days, seven days a week, assembling oil pumps and then selling oil drilling bits. While the family lived on the West coast, Barbara gave birth to George W.'s sister, Robin.

The Bush family in Midland, Texas. From left are Barbara Bush, George W. Bush, George Bush, grandmother Dorothy Walker Bush, and grandfather Prescott Bush.

In the late spring of 1950, the Bushes were transferred to Midland, Texas, 20 miles from their former home in Odessa. Midland was where white-collar workers lived and was home to engineers, lawyers, doctors, and oil company presidents.

Many young couples from different parts of the country moved to the oil town of 25,000, and the Bushes joined other families in the brand new housing development nicknamed Easter Egg Row because the houses were painted bright colors. The young people, mostly in their twenties, were optimistic in a town where fortunes rose and fell on wet or dry oil wells. Deals were made on a handshake, and a man's word was his bond.

If things weren't as progressive in Midland as they were

An oil well in Midland, Texas, where George W. Bush was raised. Bush would later work in the oil business in Midland, after earning an MBA at Harvard, and he often refers to Midland as a place that helped to form his identity. In fact, at one Republican National Convention, he invoked the one-time Midland slogan "The sky's the limit" as a philosophy that had encouraged him.

in the towns from where the transplanted folks came, the new folks dug in and changed them. In the forefront of civic pride stood the Bushes. They worked on the Little League field, so George W. would have a place to play ball; they raised money for the YMCA, where George W. could race his electric train; they headed committees for the community theater, where George W. could gain a little culture. They were also revitalizing the Republican Party in a one-party state. The Bushes served on the cancer board, the United Way board, the church board, any board that asked them. They were leaders in their community, and when it came to attending fundraisers, they often dragged the children with them, introducing George W. into a world of socializing with a hidden agenda. By watching his parents interact with others, he learned how to work a crowd.

George Bush wrote a friend that the family loved Midland. "We have had a fine year—we like Texas, the kids have been well. Robin is now walking around and Georgie has grown to be a near-man, talks dirty once in a while and occasionally swears, aged 4½. He lives in his cowboy clothes."

In spring 1951 and with financing from his uncle, George Bush started an oil business with a neighbor and worked even longer hours than before, but he still made time for his two children. Sometimes, he took George W. and his friend Randy Roden out to an oil field overnight to watch the drilling. The two boys would sleep in the back of the station wagon, waking up every couple hours to see if the strange night world of towers and lights and pipes had produced a gusher.

Life was fun for George W. in Midland. He led the neighborhood children as they roamed from house to house, roughhoused with Robin, and played pickup baseball anytime he could. He walked or road his bike to Sam Houston Elementary School, and he was proud when his grandfather was elected to the Senate. Early in 1953 he got a little brother, John Ellis Bush, called Jeb because of his initials. And then one morning things changed drastically. Robin, age three, woke up and told her mom, "I don't know what to do this morning. I may go out and lie on the grass and watch the cars go by, or I might just stay in bed." She was too tired to rush around like George W.

Barbara took Robin straight to the doctor, and by afternoon the blood test diagnosis was in. Leukemia. The doctor thought Robin would live only a few weeks, but the Bushes took her to Memorial Sloan-Kettering Hospital in New York

City for the latest treatments, and her life was lengthened by months. George Bush flew back and forth between New York and Texas, tending to his company's merger with another oil company. Barbara stayed with Robin. A nanny sent by their grandmother supervised George W. and Jeb. George W. was told that Robin was sick, but his parents chose not to tell him that Robin was dying. They feared he would tell Robin, and they also thought it was a heavy burden for a six-year-old to handle.

Robin was brought back to Midland once to visit, but George W. was told not to roughhouse with her. In the summer, the family went to Kennebunkport, and Robin was brought up there for a short while. But again there was no playing with Robin, because she could develop internal bleeding with merely a touch.

Back in Midland in the fall, George W. was carrying a phonograph back to the principal's office on a long outdoor walkway when he looked up and saw his parents' car. He thought he saw Robin in the back seat. He put down the phonograph and ran to the car. But Robin wasn't there, and his parents told him she had died.

Years later he wrote, ". . . those minutes remain the starkest memory of my childhood, a sharp pain in the midst of an otherwise happy blur."

It was hard for a seven-year-old boy to accept that his sister was gone forever. He grieved and he talked about her. He'd learned at school that the earth rotated on its axis, and he wondered if sometimes Robin was standing on her head in her grave. He commented once at a football game with his father that he wished he were Robin. "Why?" his father asked. "I bet she can see the game better from up there than we can here."

Although he believed Robin was in heaven, George W. felt a great sadness, and he experienced nightmares. The elder Bush was traveling a great deal with his new merged firm,

George W. Bush with his parents and his brothers Jeb, Neil, and Marvin in Midland, circa 1956.

Zapata Petroleum Corporation, while Barbara Bush stayed at home with the two boys. Her grief overwhelmed her, and her hair started turning white. She did not understand how responsible her oldest son felt for her until, months after Robin's death, she overheard him tell a friend that he couldn't play because his mom needed him. That shook her. She dried her tears, tucked her grief in her heart, and faced the day with a smile.

As more months passed, the Bushes adapted to life without Robin. Another brother, Neil, was born, and the family moved to a big brick home with a swimming pool. The following year, George W. gained another brother, Marvin. But George W. was much older than his brothers, nearly seven years older than Jeb, so he didn't play with them much; instead he played with friends from school and the neighborhood.

Thoughts of baseball dominated his life. He collected baseball cards, sending them off to be autographed by the players, then stacking them in a cardboard box and memorizing the stats of the ballplayers. He played catcher for the Little League team, and he dreamed of being a big league player someday.

At school George W. was a leader, and many times a spirited one, landing in his share of trouble. He once threw a football through a window into the classroom when the class had been told not to go outside at lunch break. Another time, he was sent to the principal's office for drawing an ink mustache, sideburns, and goatee on his face. He was always funny, quick with a quip, and genuinely liked his classmates.

By now the elder Bush was traveling more than ever with Zapata, leaving George W.'s mother in charge of the four boys. Her personality was a dominant force in her eldest son's life. "My mother's always been a very outspoken person who vents very well—she'll just let it rip if she's got something on her mind. Once it's over, you know exactly where you stand and that's it," George W. said later. He could have been describing his own way of reacting to life around him.

Friends liked George W.'s forthright manner, and they elected him president of the seventh grade at San Jacinto Junior High. He also played on the football team that year. His town had grown now to 65,000, and George W. had made a place in it for himself by his friendly personality just as his parents had made a place for themselves by their civic work. But George Bush's successful oil company had grown an offshore drilling arm, and he needed to be in Houston by the Gulf of Mexico.

In the summer before the eighth grade, George W. and his brothers moved to a new house in the huge city of Houston and welcomed a new little sister, Dorothy, to the family. His parents enrolled George W. in Kincaid School, an exclusive private school. He quickly made friends and was elected a class officer.

In the spring of 1961, George W. returned from school one day to be greeted by his mother. She told him congratulations; he'd been accepted at Phillips Academy in Andover, Massachusetts, the same private prep school that his father had attended.

George W.'s childhood days in Texas were coming to an end as he prepared once again to move and make new friends, but in an environment so very different from his beloved Texas.

1964 yearbook photograph of George W. Bush, Phillips Academy, Andover, Massachusetts.

3

An Eastern Education

Moving to Andover, Massachusetts, to attend Phillips Academy meant a major change in George W.'s life. Instead of the hot weather he was used to in Midland, with occasional sand storms thrown in, or the humidity of Houston from the bay, there would be frigid temperatures and snow storms.

But the weather was the least of his worries. At the age of 15 he was leaving a tight family unit to live with strangers. He knew only one person at his new school, his old friend Randy Roden from his Midland days.

Andover was an old school, established during the Revolutionary War, and very little in the way of scheduling had changed from that time. Boys in the all-male school were required to start the day early with chapel or occasionally a school assembly. Classes started promptly with demerits handed out for a student being seconds late. By early afternoon classes ended, and two to three hours of sports and organized activities began, followed by more classes until 6:00. Evenings were for studying, and lights went out at 10:00.

Besides adapting to this highly structured world, George W. wanted desperately to live up to the reputation that his father had built during his years at Andover. George Bush had excelled in academics, in sports, and in student government. He'd been named Best All-Around Fellow.

In academics, George W. started off the year on the wrong foot. When assigned an essay on an emotional experience, he wrote about Robin's death and how deeply it had moved him. In revising his work, he saw that he had overused the word *tears* (in the sense of crying), so he pulled out the new thesaurus his mother had given him and found the word *lacerates*, not realizing it was a suggested synonym for the word *tears* (in the sense of rending). His teacher gave him a failing grade and wrote "Disgraceful. See me immediately." George W. pulled up the grade, and from that point on he held his own in a very competitive academic environment.

In sports, George W. was a junior varsity caliber player in both baseball and basketball. At one tense basketball game, someone said, "Bush, get in there!" and George W. jumped up from his normal seat on the bench before laughter told him it was just a practical joke. By his final year, he was third-string varsity in baseball, but he warmed the bench more than he played.

In student government, George W. was elected representative-at-large to the Student Congress, but that was in his last year at the school, and he was never an officer. Still he was friendly, well liked, and knew most of the students by name, important characteristics for a budding politician.

Since he couldn't live up to his father's name, he decided to become a leader in a different category—frivolity. Other

George W. Bush as head cheerleader at Phillips Academy in another photograph from the 1964 yearbook.

students thought of him as a funny guy, and he earned the nickname "Lip" because he was so quick with a funny quip. He pushed the line where rules were concerned, daring the administrators to challenge his adherence to the coat and tie requirement. Sometimes he wore a tee shirt, a badly knotted tie, and an army surplus jacket to the dining hall.

Since he didn't excel in sports, George W. tackled cheerleading. By the end of his three-year stint at Andover, he was head cheerleader. The yearbook showed pictures of the cheerleading

George W.'s two brushes with legal authorities involved alcohol directly. The first occurred one December when he and other DKEs, laughing and making a lot of noise, were driving around downtown. George W. spied a wreath on a storefront and thought it would dress up the DKE house. No sooner had he taken it than patrolling New Haven police arrested him and charged him with disorderly conduct. He later referred to it as the "Christmas wreath caper." The revelers apologized and the charges were dropped.

The second incident occurred at a Yale-Princeton football game, with Yale victorious for the first time in eight years. George W., who had been drinking, and about 30 others raced on the field to tear down the wooden goalpost. Campus police grabbed him along with a handful of others, escorted them off the field, and told them to get out of town.

During his time at Yale, George W. was concerned about his father's political activities. In November of his freshman year, he went home for election night and posted voting returns as they came in to the campaign's headquarters. It was not a pleasant job. His father was defeated for the office, and George W. felt as dejected as the others in his family. It did not help that the atmosphere at Yale was very liberal and George Bush's views were rather conservative; George W. took the talk he heard on campus as personal criticism of Bush family politics. Still he followed his father's example of bouncing back, analyzing the event, knowing he gave it his best shot, and moving on.

At a time when many college students felt they had nothing in common with their parents, George W. held utmost respect for his father. That didn't keep him from making some bad judgment calls that reflected on his father. His summer job before his sophomore year was working on an inland Louisiana oil barge anchored in 20 feet of water. He worked seven to ten days on and then had seven to ten days off. During his off periods, he returned to Houston and partied

George W. Bush at Yale University; he attended Yale from 1964 until 1968.

with his friends. A week before his summer commitment was up, George W. told his fellow crew members that he wasn't coming back; he wanted to be with friends and his girlfriend in Houston. When he got back to the city, he was called to his father's office.

"You agreed to work a certain amount of time, and you didn't," his father told him. "I just want you to know that you have disappointed me."

George W. was crushed. Even though a few hours later his father asked him to accompany him to a Houston Astros game, so he obviously wasn't holding a grudge, George W. would always remember how it felt to let his father down.

The following summer when he returned to Houston, George W. took a job as a sporting goods salesman at Sears. He devoted that summer to seeing his girlfriend, Cathryn Wolfman, and helping with his father's new campaign for the United States Congress from Texas's Seventh District.

In November, George W. returned to Houston from Yale for "Reality Day," the Bush term for Election Day. This time when he posted the voting results, there was reason for whoops and yells. George Bush had been elected to Congress.

Before his father could assume his congressional seat in Washington, D.C., at the January swearing-in, George W. had made a big decision about his own life. He gave an engagement ring to Cathryn for Christmas, but they did not set a wedding date, although they planned to marry the summer before his senior year. They talked long-distance during the spring semester, postponed the wedding, but continued to see each other the following summer, while George W. worked as a bookkeeper for a securities firm. When no plan had been made by his senior year, he figured the wedding was off, but their engagement wasn't officially ended for several more months.

Talk among Yale's 1968 graduating seniors, the last all-male class at Yale, centered on the war in Vietnam and their student draft deferments that would change the moment they graduated college. Some anti-war seniors talked of heading to Canada to avoid the draft; some enrolled in medical school; a few signed up for the military. Bush enlisted in the Texas Air National Guard.

He wanted to return to Texas where people were friendly. He looked forward to getting away from what he called the intellectual snobs at school; he had never fit into the anti-establishment mood during those turbulent times. He just wanted to go home to Texas.

In this image from 1968, George W. Bush, left, has been made an officer in the Texas Air National Guard. His father, George H.W. Bush, pins on his son's insignia.

4

Finding His Way

There was talk that George W. had a few strings pulled to get into the Texas Air National Guard, where open slots were rare. It was a fairly safe way of being in the military while avoiding active duty in Vietnam, where an unpopular war raged. Sons of influential people flocked to sign up and do their patriotic duty stateside in the Guard. George Bush denied that he asked anyone to help his son get a coveted spot. George W. says he wanted to be a pilot like his father, was accepted because he passed the pilot tests, and found an open slot because few men were willing to sign away the six years necessary for flight training and weekend duties. Later, a Bush family friend admitted, although he had not been asked to do it, that he made a call to the general in charge of the Guard informing him that Congressman Bush's son was trying to get into that branch of the military.

George W. spent basic training, five hot summer weeks, at Lackland Air Force Base in San Antonio. Upon completion, he was to report to a base in Houston until his Air Force flight training began in November. A couple weeks after he finished basic, he was granted leave to work on a political campaign in Florida until after Election Day in November, returning to Houston occasionally for weekend duty.

George W. worked as an aid for the senatorial campaign of Congressman Edward J. Gurney of Florida. George W.'s job was to herd press corps members on and off the campaign plane and get them into hotel rooms. This responsibility gave him experiences in handling difficult pressroom situations using his trademark humor and brazen straightforward manner of dealing with people.

Second lieutenant George W. analyzed the campaign, which was hard-fought and an uphill battle for the conservative Gurney. The politician focused on three issues. He hammered them over and over and was not detoured by side issues. He did not soften his position, and once he won the election, Gurney said partisan politics were set aside now for the good of the people, and he'd work toward implementing his three issues. George W. noted how effective the focused approach worked. Gurney never wavered from his message, and by observing this politician, George W. learned how to wage a winning campaign.

Toward the end of November, George W. arrived at Moody Air Force Base in Valdosta, Georgia. Among some 70 pilot trainees, George W. was the only Guardsman; the others were regular military. George W. actually did very well in pilot school. His remarkable memory served him in good stead where charts and diagrams were involved. But a few trainees felt George W. received preferential treatment from instructors because they were after promotions and thought they might get recommendations from Congressman Bush.

Joe Chaney, an airman from Alabama, said that everyone

Bush in the cockpit of a jet fighter in 1968. At the time, he was a lieutenant in the Texas Air National Guard, stationed at Ellington Field near Houston.

knew who George W. Bush was and knew that his father was a congressman, but George W. never put on airs. Chancy said, "We worked hard and played hard, throwing dice and talking about flying and drinking. We went to the bar, played bar games, swapped lies. He was extremely intelligent, very witty and humorous."

Midway thorough training, other pilot trainees watched as a government plane landed from Andrews Air Force Base, picked up George W., and flew him to Washington. President Nixon had ordered the plane because his daughter, Tricia, needed a dinner date. When he returned to his base, George W.

refused to give details about the date except to say it wasn't very long. The others were amazed that he could leave the base, when they were stuck in the summer heat of Georgia.

In December 1969 pilot training was over, and George W. and half his classmates earned their wings. He headed back to Houston for an assignment flying night maneuvers out of Ellington Air Force Base. Because he was a congressman's son, the Texas Air National Guard used George W. in one of its promotional ads, claiming he got his kicks from flying a jet.

He also got his kicks from fun and was in the center of activity at the singles apartment complex where he lived. He drank beer with other tenants, played volleyball in one of the six swimming pools, and dated extensively. He lived in a cluttered apartment (clothes and cans on the floor) and drove a cluttered car (clothes and papers on the seats), but he lived a fairly uncluttered life.

A few months remained before George W. completed the two-year active duty phase of his training. His father was running for the Senate again, and this time George W. was an occasional member of the campaign team, flying off on one-day jaunts. Wearing his National Guard flight jacket, he would step to the microphone and say a few words of praise for his father.

In June, George W. began his four-year inactive duty, which required that he fly the F-102 jet only a few times a month. At loose ends the rest of the time, he joined his father's campaign, traveling across the state with a busload of college interns and speaking on behalf of his father. He described his role as "surrogate candidate," since he addressed the many, many issues exactly as his conservative father did, without regard to his own opinions that were more moderate.

George Bush lost the Senate race to Lloyd Bentsen, and George W. heard charges of carpetbagger because of his father's Eastern roots and Ivy League education. George W. took the loss hard, even though his father was quickly appointed to the prestigious job of ambassador to the United Nations.

George W., now a first lieutenant, reported one weekend a month to the base, which allowed plenty of time for him to pursue a career, but he had no specific direction. He drifted along, visiting his parents in New York City and attending Mets games while there, courtesy of his great uncle, who was part owner.

He applied to law school at the University of Texas, but was turned down, and what he called his "nomadic period" began with a series of short-term jobs, obtained through his father's contacts. He signed on with Stratford of Texas, an agricultural development company, as a management trainee who learned to prepare reports, give presentations, and nego-tiate purchase agreements for horticultural operations in the United States and in Central America. After nine months on the job, he knew that was not the type of career he wanted and he resigned.

Between jobs, he toyed with the idea of running for a legislative position in the Texas House or Senate. *The Houston Post* ran a short article about George W. pondering the possibility. But after a talk with his father, who told him he didn't yet have the experience to run, he decided against the idea.

Instead, he followed his father's advice and took a job as political director on the senate campaign of Winton M. Blount in Alabama. Here he could learn more of the ins and outs of campaigning. He set up rallies, handed out literature, and met with Republican workers in small towns. He watched the candidates give speeches and also noted how Blount's opponent was much more personable with the public. Blount stayed on his message, hitting his main issues, but he didn't have the personality to converse with the voters

Winton Blount, Postmaster General–designate in the Nixon administration, photographed in December of 1968.

on a personal level. It was no surprise that George W.'s boss was beaten at the polls.

While he worked on the campaign, George W. put in his weekend flying time with the 187th Tactical Reconnaissance Group in Montgomery, Alabama, and after the election, he returned to flying out of his home base in Houston. Once again he was out of a fulltime job.

On a Christmas trip to visit his family in Washington, D.C., where his father was now serving as chairman of the Republican Party, George W. caroused with friends. One evening he took his younger brother Marvin with him, and the two imbibed. Driving home, George W. hit a neighbor's trashcan, which stuck to the wheel of his car. The banging noise continued until he parked in his parents' driveway. Once they were in the house and the family saw the state of 15-year-old Marvin, George Bush called his oldest son into the den.

"I hear you're looking for me," said an inebriated George W. "You wanna go *mano a mano* right here?"

His brother Jeb stepped in to defuse the situation. He announced that George W. had been accepted at Harvard Business School. George Bush told his son he should seriously consider that, but George W. countered with a statement that he wasn't going; he just wanted to see if he could get in.

He'd been accepted, but it was for the fall of 1973, nine months away. To fill the gap, he took yet another job that his father recommended. While still flying for the Guard, George W. began working for the Professional United Leadership League (PULL), an organization that linked famous athletes and celebrities with Houston's inner-city kids. George W. worked on public relations, fundraising, and mentoring the children. Senior counselor Muriel Simmons Henderson remembered him: "He never put himself in the position of looking down his nose at someone, like 'I've got all this money, my father is George Bush.' He never talked about his father. He was so down to earth. You could not help liking him. He was always fun."

One kid especially, kindergartner Jimmy Dean, hung on George W.'s every word and also hung on his leg or his arm, following him like a shadow. When the tough boy would show up without shoes or a shirt, George W. took him shopping. Much later George W. learned that as a teen Jimmy was killed by gunfire.

At this job in urban Houston, George W. saw a different part of life than the country club and private school set he was accustomed to seeing. He made a difference in children's lives, and he liked helping them.

When his term started at Harvard, George W. requested an early discharge from the Texas Air National Guard. His enlistment period was not up until May 1974, but he was given early release and transferred to a reserve unit in Boston. His military file said:

"Lt. Bush's major strength is his ability to work with others. Lt. Bush is very active in civic affairs in the community and manifests a deep interest in the operation of our government."

He was also deeply interested in how business organizations worked. Harvard Business School taught through case studies of businesses, what went wrong, and how to fix them. Reading a hundred to three hundred pages a day and writing a paper a week took time and energy, and George W. settled down to learn all he could.

He still had fun; he would not have been himself if he hadn't enjoyed the people around him. He befriended other students, played intramural baseball and softball, and drank at local bars, favoring a country-western bar that reminded him of Texas. In a time when there was lots of antiwar, anti-Nixon, anti-establishment feelings on campus, he proudly wore his National Guard flight jacket. In his yearbook picture, he wore a rumpled sports shirt, not a coat and tie. He didn't fit in, but it didn't bother him. His friend April Foley told a reporter:

> This was HBS and people were fooling around with the accouterments of money and power. While they were drinking Chivas Regal, he was drinking Wild Turkey. They were smoking Benson and Hedges and he's dipping Copenhagen, and while they were going to the opera he was listening to Johnny Rodriguez over and over and over and over.

By the time he graduated from Harvard's Business School, George W. had determined that the place to make a fortune was in his own back yard, Midland, Texas. Another oil boom beckoned him to his childhood home. Before he started west, he detoured for a few weeks vacation to China, where his father was now chief of the U.S. Liaison Office. George W. enjoyed the family and the sightseeing, but it was time for him to establish a life for himself.

Armed with around $15,000 seed money left over from his Bush-Walker education fund, he set his sights on Midland with the plan of learning the oil business. He was setting out on his own, but he was once again following in his father's footsteps.

George W. Bush talks with workers while campaigning for Congress in the Midland oil fields in this 1978 photo. In 1978, 32-year-old George W. Bush had moved back to Midland, his childhood home, and entered the oil business. Midland was at the southern end of the sprawling 19th Congressional District.

5

The Family Business

idland was all he thought it would be: hot, dusty, and home. Several of George W.'s childhood friends had returned to Midland after starting careers in bigger cities, so he had a circle of friends from his first days back in West Texas, and he made new ones, too.

George W. quickly formed bonds with Don Evans, Charlie Younger, and Joe O'Neill, who would remain lifelong friends. George W. was known as a friendly guy, but he qualified exactly what a friend was. A friend was "someone who is loyal. An acquaintance is some-one who might not be loyal. Loyal means that I'm with you when times are good or times are bad."

With his typical housekeeping ways, George W. turned his rented two-room guesthouse into a bachelor pad with newspapers and clothes on the floor. His bed frame was held together with neckties, which he figured was a much better use for them than around his neck.

Many of his parents' old friends still lived in the oil town, and George W. turned to them for advice on starting his new life. Be a land man, they told him. Serving as the middleman between oil drillers and landowners was the place to start in the oil business, and it was a natural choice for a history major trained in research.

George W. went to the courthouse and looked up deeds. He was concerned with who owned the surface of the land, and he was just as interested in who owned the earth below. Farmers would sell off mineral rights to certain depths. One oil company could own down to approximately 5,000 feet. Another might own mineral rights from 5,001 to 8,000 feet, and another company could own the rights down another thousand feet. Land ownership was stratified.

Once he determined who owned land in the unmarked, unfenced dry Texas land and checked many handwritten deeds to see who owned oil and gas rights, it was time to knock on doors of farmhouses and talk to farmers about selling their mineral rights. George W. would firmly shake hands while looking the owner straight in the eyes. He'd talk about the weather, discuss the local high school football team, and finally get around to talking about oil.

The job was actually linking together different types of people and persuading them that they wanted to connect in a business deal. As he had done in school, as stickball commissioner and fraternity president, he learned the needs of the men involved and coordinated action. The land man job let him be his own boss.

"I wasn't about to do something that I didn't want to do. I was single. My overhead was extremely low. I knew I didn't want to work for anybody for a while," he later told a reporter for the *Dallas Morning News.*

Money he earned from working as a land man kept

George W. financially solvent. He rationed out his seed money from the Walker-Bush fund and lived on a shoestring budget. He wore hand-me-down shirts from a friend; he drove a car that needed a paint job; and he used Scotch tape to repair his loafers. As a practical joke to point out his skinflint ways, a friend took old Christmas cards from an oil company, crossed off the name, and forged George W. Bush's signature. People around Midland chuckled when they received the recycled Christmas cards.

George W. had fun with his friends, too. He jogged most mornings, and when he passed an old oilman on the track, he pulled down the man's running shorts and zipped right past him. He and Charlie Younger went to nearby Odessa, drank a little too much, and climbed onstage behind Willie Nelson and sang along. Once he decided to take Don Evans flying in a rented Cessna. George W. checked out the plane, climbed inside, and discovered he didn't know how to fly it. When he finally got it started, he lifted the nose straight up as he would a jet and nearly stalled the plane. He managed a wobbly landing. Then, as if the first attempt had never happened, he asked Don if he wanted to fly around Midland. This time he took off, flew around a bit, and landed for the final time. He never flew a plane again.

He attended backyard barbeques, cheered on the minor-league Midland Angels, and played touch football. He didn't forget the civic responsibility lessons that his parents had taught him by example: he volunteered for the United Way, he taught Sunday school, and he supported the Republican Party.

After a year in Midland, he invested a little bit in wells drilled by others. The self-proclaimed "Mr. Frugal" was baffled when the first well was dry. This oil business was not going to be as easy as he had anticipated. He'd invested a few thousand, and then it was gone. But the next well and the next one dribbled some oil, so he made up his loss and added a bit to his bank account.

As content as he seemed, something was missing—politics. Of course, he was in touch with his father's political life. When President Gerald Ford appointed George Bush director of the CIA, he asked George W. to canvass his siblings in order to find out how they would feel about him taking the job since there would surely be a lot of criticism. George W. wrote him, "I look forward to the opportunities to hold my head high and declare ever so proudly that yes, George Bush, super spook, is my Dad and that yes I am damn glad for my country that he is head of the agency."

EARLY DAYS IN POLITICS

The opportunity to enter politics in his own right came when incumbent Congressman George Mahon decided not to run for reelection. The 19th District was now wide open, and George W. threw his hat in the ring. His friends told him that money would be no problem and to leave the fundraising to them. Don Evans volunteered as campaign chair.

George W.'s experience in his father's campaigns in Texas and the ones in Florida and Alabama had taught him a thing or two about campaigns. He wanted to start early, and he wanted to remain focused on a few critical issues. Midland, Odessa, and Lubbock were the three towns of any size in the district. The first two were oil towns, and George W. expected to do well in those areas. Agricultural interests controlled Lubbock, and he knew little about farm problems, but he told folks he was ready to learn and would represent them well.

In July 1977, well over a year before the election, George W. announced he would be seeking the congressional seat. A couple weeks later his plans were sidelined temporarily by a most unexpected event. His friends Joe and Jan O'Neill asked him to a backyard barbeque, and they also invited Jan's former roommate, Laura Welch, who was in Midland visiting her parents.

Laura grew up in Midland and attended school at

William Colby applauds his successor, and President Gerald Ford looks on, as George H.W. Bush finishes remarks after his swearing-in as director of the Central Intelligence Agency (CIA), January 30, 1976, in Washington.

Southern Methodist University in Dallas. After graduation, she taught elementary school in Houston and lived in the very same apartment complex where George W. had an apartment while he was in the Guard. However, he lived in the noisy section, and she lived at the opposite end on the quite side, so their paths never crossed.

Reading was Laura's passion, and she delighted in reading to her students. This pastime led her to pursue a master's degree in library science from the University of Texas in Austin. For a while she served as a children's librarian in Houston, then she returned to Austin to work as a librarian in an elementary school. She visited her parents in Midland quite often, and whenever she saw her former roommate, Jan O'Neill, O'Neill would ask if she'd like to meet George W.

Laura knew who he was and remembered him from his grammar school days in Midland, but each time the invitation was extended, she declined. She was aware of the Bush legacy, and she wasn't interested in politics. Finally, one summer day, she accepted and re-met her future husband.

On the outside, the two were opposite. As a reporter later wrote, George W., nicknamed "The Bombastic Bushkin" by his friends, was the type that a librarian would tell to be quiet. But on the inside, the two held very similar values: love of family, respect for others' opinions, and loyalty to friends. After that first evening, Laura told her mother that she liked George W. because he made her laugh. George W. told his parents that he had met a woman who was a great listener, and since he was a great talker, they were a good fit. George W. Bush wrote about Laura in his book *A Charge to Keep*:

> We are not really opposite, although we are different. Laura is naturally reserved; I am outgoing. Laura stays in her own space; I've always invaded other people's spaces, leaning into them, touching, hugging, getting close. Some might mistake her calm for shyness, but they are wrong. She is totally at ease, comfortable and natural, just calm. I, on the other hand, am perpetual motion. I provoke people, confront them in a teasing way. I pick at a problem, drawing it to the surface. She is kinder, much more measured, arriving at a conclusion carefully, yet certainly.

Three months after they met, they married in a simple church ceremony in Midland. They had both served in several big weddings, and they decided they didn't want to plan a huge event. Neither one had attendants, but they had their families and closest friends to witness their vows.

Laura made George W. promise that she would not have to give a public speech as his congressional campaign heated up.

George W. Bush and his wife, Laura Bush, shown on a campaign poster from around 1978.

But three months later, he told her he had a scheduling conflict, and asked her to fill in for him in Muleshoe, Texas. The speech was a test of endurance for her, and she ran out of words.

Laura learned the hard way to take her mother-in-law's advice. Barbara Bush had suggested that she never criticize her husband's speeches. One night when they were pulling into their drive, George W. asked Laura how his speech had gone. When she told him it wasn't very good, he was so dumbfounded, he drove into the garage wall.

GEORGE BUSH FOR CONGRESS

George W. won the Republican nomination over ex-mayor of Odessa Jim Reese and set his sights on the general election. His opponent, Democrat Kent Hance, was from the Lubbock area and had the strong backing of agricultural interests. His campaign blasted George W. as a transplanted Easterner. Hance later bragged that George W. had one of the finest educations available and he had turned it against him. George W.'s first big television ad showed him jogging, symbolic of a man of action. Again Hance turned that against him. West Texans didn't jog for exercise; they worked the fields.

Unbeknownst to George W., in September a college intern had placed an ad in the Texas Tech student paper announcing a "Bush Bash" with music and free beer. Five days before the November election, a letter from Hance's former law partner was mailed to 4,000 anti-alcohol church members. Staffers wanted George W. to denounce Hance as a hypocrite because he was one owner of land that rented to a nightclub, but George W. didn't want negative campaigning. He later said he regretted that decision. "When someone attacks your integrity, you have to respond."

Much later, a Bush staffer ran into a Democrat who had worked for Hance, who told her that he had written the "Bush Bash" ad and that the college intern had been on the Democrats' payroll. If this is true—and other Democrats say it was a possibility—then it was George W.'s first encounter with dirty politics, though certainly not his last.

On election night, George W. carried the oil areas, but lost Lubbock and the rural areas. Of course he was disappointed, but he remembered that his father and his grandfather had lost their first elections, too.

Out of politics, George W. poured his energies into his new oil company, Arbusto, Spanish for *bush*. His uncle Jonathan

Bush helped him set up a limited partnership that would draw investors. With his uncle's Wall Street connections and his own ability as a salesman drawn from his land man days, George W. put together a sizeable group of investors and began drilling. Some holes were dry, some held oil, none were the gushers George W. hoped for, but managing the company taught George W. that hiring intelligent capable men and trusting them to do their jobs was the way to instill loyalty in employees.

As well as working for himself, he was also working part-time for his father's campaign for president. When George W. spoke on his father's behalf, he swaggered to the podium, hit the major points, and sat down. He wore boots that showed he was Western through and through, but he occasionally misjudged his audience. When he was speaking in the East, he was seen as too rough, but in Texas he was becoming one of the boys.

Ronald Reagan beat George Bush on the road to the Republican convention, but Reagan selected him as his vice presidential running mate, and the subsequent election was an overwhelming Republican victory. With his father as vice president, George W. put his own political ambitions aside. He did not want to run on his father's coattails.

Other events were capturing his time. Laura was pregnant with twins, and in the last trimester, she suffered from toxemia. She was hospitalized seven weeks before the due date, but the toxemia worsened, and she delivered twins Barbara and Jenna, named for their grandmothers, five weeks before they were due. George W. was in the room during the cesarean section on November 25, 1981, and he called it the "most thrilling moment of my life."

His personal life was at a peak, but his business was starting a downward slide. The price of oil was dropping, and the jokes around Midland about "Ar-*bust*-o" provoked George W. enough to change the name of his company to Bush

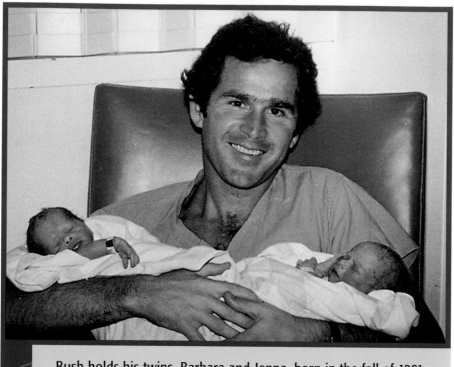

Bush holds his twins, Barbara and Jenna, born in the fall of 1981 in Dallas.

Exploration. The new name couldn't halt the downward price spiral or the dry wells, and in 1984, George W. merged his company with successful Spectrum 7. Part of the deal was stock in the company, and he was retained as chairman.

Now he was back in the business of finding investors, and he again used his land man training to strike a deal. Many days he'd leave the house at the crack of dawn, fly out of the Midland airport, and meet with investors that his uncle Jonathan had chosen. But widespread investors couldn't stop the price of oil from sinking even lower. Two years later Spectrum 7 was in financial trouble, but another buyout, this time by Harken Energy, saved George W. Again he was paid in shares, he was named a director of the company, and he was hired as a consultant for investor relations.

George W. worked hard and played hard. As he approached his 40th birthday, he and Laura and some friends planned a getaway weekend in Colorado Springs, Colorado. After a night of heavy drinking, George W. rose early and set out for his morning run, but he had a hangover and his energy was sapped. When he made it back to the hotel, he told Laura that he was through with drinking. And that was that. He didn't make a big event of it. He continued to go to parties but he just didn't drink. He felt more energetic, more focused, and more disciplined than before. He claimed, "It is one of the best things I have ever done."

He claimed the seeds were sown for the change a year earlier when he'd had a spiritual reawakening. The Reverend Billy Graham had visited the Bush family at the annual August family reunion in Maine. George W. talked at length with the evangelist and returned to Midland to read and study the Bible. His growth as a Christian helped him make the decision to quit drinking.

His father also weighed heavily in the decision. George Bush was making a run for the presidency, and George W. didn't want to do anything that would embarrass his father.

Bush, son of the Vice President, stands with Texas Governor Bill Clements Jr. in New Orleans, August 18, 1988. Bush waved a flag after casting the Texas delegation's vote, which secured his father's nomination as the GOP (Grand Old Party) presidential candidate.

6

The President's Son

George W. felt that timing was everything, and 1988 was the time for his father to run for president. History books showed that many vice presidents had not been elected president, and George W. wanted to make sure that his father had every chance to succeed.

Campaign political advisors control a great deal of what Americans perceive as a candidate's image. George Bush had selected brash and innovative Lee Atwater to steer his campaign. At a meeting in 1986 at Camp David, the government retreat, the vice president called his family together to meet his team of advisors. George W. and brother Jeb wondered about Atwater's loyalties since his political consulting firm was also courting other presidential candidates as clients.

"How do we know we can trust you?" George W. asked flat out.

Jeb seconded the question. "What he means is, if someone throws a grenade at our dad, we expect you to jump on it."

"If you're so worried about my loyalty, why don't you come to Washington and help me with the campaign?" Atwater asked. "That way if there's a problem, you'll be there to solve it."

George W. accepted the challenge. In the spring of 1987, he and Laura sold their Midland home and moved the family to Washington. George W. became the loyalty enforcer for the campaign. His father appreciated the devotion and wrote in his diary:

> I think [his] coming up here will be very helpful and I think he will be a good insight to me. He is very level-headed, and so is Jebby. I think some of our political people are thinking, "Oh, God, here come the Bush boys." But, you know where their loyalty is and they both have excellent judgment and they are both spending a bunch of time on this project.

George W. had no official title, but he had access to the candidate whenever he wanted it. He decided which reporters could have private interviews with his father, appeared at Republican Party fundraisers, and courted the Christian right, the fundamentalist groups that controlled a large block of voters. Those people who couldn't gain access to the candidate felt if they talked to George W., he would make their opinions known to his father.

He served the same type of role with the campaign staff. He listened to one opinion and then another, sorted through the problem, and reported to his father in a straightforward manner. He learned to listen, he learned to evaluate, and he learned to communicate.

George Bush had not yet declared his candidacy when an unsubstantiated rumor, which was untrue, was started about an alleged affair with a staffer. Atwater's plan was to respond. He leaked the story that George W. had asked his father point-blank and been told no. By quoting George W.'s quip, "The answer to the Big A question is N.O.," to a reporter who printed it, Atwater defused the issue and got the campaign, a campaign that was not yet official, moving forward again. George W., who carefully watched Atwater's movements, learned how to handle a sticky situation.

In October 1987 George Bush announced he was running for president. The press conference went well, but the accompanying *Newsweek* cover story caused an explosion inside George W. He had given the reporter access to the candidate, even invited her to Maine to be with the family, and the thanks she showed was in the cover headline, "Fighting the Wimp Factor." George Bush wrote in his diary, "That *Newsweek* story was the cheapest shot I've seen in my political life."

George W. was furious and berated the reporter. After all, his father had been the youngest pilot in the Navy, had been shot down and rescued, and this reporter had dared to use the word "wimp." The candidate's gentlemanly manners were being held against him. Through the rest of the primary campaign, George W. held reporters at arm's length and was known as the "Roman candle" of the Bush camp. He sparked and exploded when his father was attacked. He became the gatekeeper for reporters to pass through, and he wanted to check their material for accuracy.

He continued to watch Lee Atwater, gaining more respect for and learning all he could from the master strategist. Atwater maintained that a cool persona was critical and that George W. needed to curtail his temper. George W. agreed and worked at calming down his feisty manner.

But again he was livid when, from the podium of the Democratic National Convention, Texas State Treasurer Ann Richards made fun of his father. "Poor George, he was born with a silver foot in his mouth." The often-quoted remark

Political strategist Lee Atwater and Republican presidential nominee George H.W. Bush at a campaign rally during the 1988 presidential race.

made Barbara Bush physically ill, and George W., never one to take lightly any criticism of his father, put Richards on his mental blacklist.

By convention time, George Bush had enough votes to win the Republican nomination. George W.'s siblings announced the vote in their states when the roll call was taken: Neil in Colorado, Jeb in Florida, Doro in Maine, and Marvin in Virginia. Although the roll call was in alphabetical order, several states passed so that George W. could announce the delegate vote in Texas that sealed the nomination. As he cast the 111 Texas delegate votes, George W. said, "For a man we respect and a man we love, for her favorite son and the best father in America . . . the man who made me proud every single day of my life and a man who will make America proud, the next president of the United States."

During the campaign, George W. continued in the role he'd played before the nomination. He kept faithful watch over his father, and he continued to observe Atwater's brand of campaigning, facing every dirty political rumor as if it were a balloon and pricking a hole in it.

Before the election, George W. received a call from an old friend from his Spectrum 7 days. The Texas Rangers baseball team was for sale; of course, George W. was interested. But it took time to find investors for such a big venture. Others across the country were also interested in the team, so George W. quickly resorted to his organizational training as an oil land man and made lists of prospects.

George W. knew he was going back to Texas after the election. He was still a consultant for Harken Energy, which was headquartered in Dallas, and Texas was home. A few days after his father was elected president, he closed on a house in north Dallas. George W. and his family stayed in Washington while he served on the Scrub Team, the committee that decided which people deserved jobs in the White

House, but by mid-December a moving truck was taking their belongings back to Texas.

Inauguration Day found George W. and family back in Washington watching the parade from the presidential viewing stand. As the University of Texas band marched toward them, George W. put on a ten-gallon hat and grinned a grin as big as Texas.

Campaigning was in his blood, and George W. had never given up the desire to serve in an elected capacity. Now he set his sights on the governorship of Texas in 1990. He ran the idea by a few people and was told he needed a bigger statewide profile and he needed to do something on his own, like his father had when he left the East and settled in Texas. He wasn't convinced 1990 wasn't good timing for him, and to make his name known, George W. took a swing around the state, speaking at Lincoln Day festivities and working for the Republican Party.

THE TEXAS RANGERS

Meanwhile he was making phone calls about the Texas Rangers. He had Eastern connections through his uncle, just as he'd had in his oil business, but the baseball commissioner wanted more of the purchase price from Texas investors. With help from the commissioner, who convinced a Texas multi-millionaire to invest, the deal was completed by spring 1989, and George W., who had made the least financial contribution and owned only 1.8% of the team, was named managing general partner who would draw a salary as the public relations man. He felt his campaign experience had taught him how to deal with the media, especially now that he had tamed his temper.

George W. was in seventh heaven; he was actually getting paid to watch baseball. He'd spent his childhood memorizing player statistics; now he mingled with ballplayers at the park, including standout pitcher Nolan Ryan. George W.

Vice President George H.W. Bush and his family acknowledge applause at the Republican National Convention in New Orleans in August of 1988. The GOP named Bush as its presidential candidate.

invited First Lady Barbara Bush to throw out the first pitch in May. She wore a Rangers jacket and posed for pictures with her son. George W. later commented:

> My mother is very good at getting and sending a message to average Americans, and that is because she is just herself. She is funny, she is glib. There's nothing phony about Barbara Bush.

His mother was a huge publicity asset to George W. in Texas, and baseball was an opportunity to become known across the state as a successful businessman. George W. sat in the stands beside the Rangers dugout in full view of TV cameras instead of sitting high in a relatively hidden owner's box. He had baseball cards made up with his picture to hand out to the crowd, and he autographed them whenever someone asked. He roved the stadium, shaking hands, patting people on the back, and learning the names of the employees, from ticket takers to hotdog vendors.

He still wanted to run for governor in 1990, but Barbara Bush mentioned to a reporter that George W. had better concentrate on baseball for a while. George W. said publicly that his mom was still giving advice out of love and concern for her son. Although off the record he was upset, he reset his sights on the 1994 race.

He had plenty of other business on his mind. Harken had been given the lease to drill offshore of Bahrain in the Persian Gulf, and although George W. was not involved in the negotiations, he was the president's son, and his name as a stockholder carried weight. When a big investor approached him to buy Harken stock, George W. saw an opportunity to sell his shares and pay his baseball team debt owed to a Midland bank. He consulted a Harken lawyer about the ethics of the deal and received the go-ahead to sell. His sale came shortly before the company announced a second-quarter loss of millions, and his deal drew criticism

Bush talks to reporters at Arlington Stadium on April 18, 1989 after the owners of both the American League and the National League approved the sale of the Texas Rangers to a group headed in part by Bush.

when it was disclosed. As a stockholder, he was required to file paperwork with the Securities and Exchange Commission. He filed his intent to sell with the SEC, and he claimed he filed a separate form for an internal sale, but the SEC said they couldn't find it. They said he filed nearly eight months after the filing deadline, and the missing paperwork that was filed on time never surfaced. A short investigation followed but was eventually dropped.

Meanwhile the United States was embroiled in Operation Desert Storm, helping Kuwait drive the Iraqi forces of Saddam Hussein out of their country. George Bush's popularity soared as the war was broadcast almost bullet by bullet on television during the short military operation. It looked like he would be a shoo-in for reelection, so the first son wouldn't be needed as the loyalty enforcer during the campaign.

George W. was invited to the White House on numerous occasions. He once attended a quiet lunch with his family and Queen Elizabeth II of England. Barbara Bush told the queen that she'd placed George W. far away from her and he was told not to say a word. The Queen asked if he was the black sheep of the family, and George W. said he guessed he was. Barbara Bush explained that George W. was dangerous because he said what he felt.

George W. tended to baseball business, and part of it was political. He helped convince the people of Arlington, where the Rangers were based, that a new stadium was absolutely necessary. They voted to raise the sales tax to foot the bill, and in April 1992 George W. drove a front-end loader and tore out a piece of the old parking lot to launch the construction of the new stadium.

That summer, George W. resigned his position on the board at Harken and devoted his extra time to his father's campaign. Things weren't going well. Third party candidate, billionaire Ross Perot, was courting conservative voters from the president, and Democrat Bill Clinton was climbing higher in the polls.

The president's campaign suffered from Lee Atwater's absence. The master strategist had died from cancer the year before, and there was no one campaign worker who could focus the campaign. George W. saw that too little was being done too late. Before election day, polls showed that George Bush would not be reelected.

Oddly enough, his father's exit from politics cleared the way for George W.'s political career. Now the timing was right.

Bush on November 4, 1992, at the Texas Rangers' new ballpark in Arlington, Texas. A few days later, Bush officially launched his campaign for governor.

7

The Governor

After his move to Dallas in 1988, George W. had contacted state party leaders, especially the big money Republicans in urban areas. Even after his father's defeat in 1992, he kept these political connections open, but George W., who rarely let his spirits get down, allowed personal problems to weigh heavily on his shoulders and push his political goals to the back of his mind.

Of course, the presidential defeat bothered him, as did the SEC inquiry into his sold shares of Harken Energy. There was trouble at the ballpark over minority contracts. His brother Neil had been sued by the federal government over a savings and loan that had gone under, and he was eventually fined $50,000. It seemed that whatever his siblings were doing was reported in the media with a negative spin. His grandmother had died shortly after the election, so his mind was enveloped in grief as well as muddled with problems that needed solutions.

Always energetic, always on the move, George W. decided to train for a marathon race. Every day he worked at the long distance goal, and in January 1993 he completed a 26-mile Houston marathon in 3 hours and 45 minutes. He had achieved his goal, and he returned to Dallas a more positive person and focused on where he wanted to go, and that was to the governor's mansion.

Through the spring, friends from Midland and Austin came to Dallas for closed-door hours-long sessions; they discussed the possibility of unseating Governor Ann Richards, the former state treasurer who on national television had belittled George Bush with her silver foot remark. Ann Richards was a character, an outspoken grandmother who liked motorcycles, and was popular with Texans.

George W. was confident he could win. Laura was less optimistic. She asked him to make certain that he wasn't being pushed into the run by others, but really wanted to tackle this campaign. She was still not excited about life in the political arena.

By late summer, the decision was made, and George W. began choosing good, loyal people to take on roles in the campaign. He turned to political consultant Karl Rove to mastermind the campaign; he chose Joe Allbaugh of Oklahoma to serve as campaign manager; he convinced Karen Hughes, executive director of the Republican Party of Texas, to resign that job and sign on as his communications director; he hired lawyer Vance McMahan to work on policy by researching the candidate's philosophic ideas and translating them into specific changes to the law.

The Bush Team christened the campaign plane *Accountability One* and decided early that the campaign would be centered on four main issues: tort reform, to do away with multimillion-dollar liability settlements; juvenile crime and how to deal with juvenile offenders; education, giving local governments control over schools; and welfare reform, getting recipients trained for jobs and forcing "deadbeat dads" to pay child support. From years earlier working on the senate campaign of Edward Gurney in Florida, George W. had seen the power of picking a few points and hammering them home over and over. He never lost sight of that during the campaign.

Team Bush decided to hit the rural areas in the first months of 1994, reserving the cities for the fall when the campaign would swing into high gear. By day, George W. shook hands at factories, schools, courthouses, and in the evenings he held fundraisers. He was a bit stiff at podiums, but when it came to working a crowd, his big grin and friendly manner took over. He delighted in meeting the people.

Not wanting to detract from George W., George and Barbara Bush were notably missing from the campaign during the first few months. But in March they attended two big fundraisers for George W. and then flew to Florida to fundraise for their second son, Jeb, who was running for governor in that state. Each candidate mentioned in speeches, although Jeb said it first, that he was not running because he was George and Barbara's son, but because he was his children's father. They were both looking to the future, not looking back.

George W. reaffirmed that the view was forward, not backward, by refusing to answer a reporter's question on whether he had experimented with drugs, a standard question asked of politicians who came of age in the turbulent '60s. "What I did as a kid? I don't think it's relevant, nor do I think it's relevant what Ann Richards did as a kid. I just don't think it matters. Did I behave irresponsibly as a kid at times? Sure did. You bet."

George W. pounded on the issues in speech after speech. Ann Richards resorted to an attack on her opponent by nicknaming him "Shrub," implying that he was the son of a Bush; she called him "Prince George" and "some jerk." She attacked his business history and reiterated the message that he'd never held public office before.

In the fall, George W. went on a dove hunt, a tradition for candidates. When his guide shouted, "Dove," George W. shot and killed the bird as cameras and reporters captured the moment. He proudly held up the bird. Unfortunately, he discovered later, the dove was actually a killdee, a protected species. He immediately called to report it, paid the $130 fine, and at his next news conference told the story and joked, "Thank goodness it was not deer season; I might have shot a cow." The Bush Team had thought the public might react negatively, but the killdee incident became a non-issue because George W. faced it head-on.

Election night found George W., Laura, and the 12-year-old twins headed to a victory celebration in Austin. His 53% win over Richards was the biggest margin in a governor's race in 20 years. His brother Jeb didn't fare as well in Florida and called his opponent to concede.

Now the work began. The governor's position in Texas government is not the most powerful in the state. George W. had a bully pulpit to make his views known and steer his agenda, and he had veto power over legislation, requiring a two-thirds vote to override. He also appointed the Secretary of State, the parole board, and commissioners of various agencies, which controlled management of the state, but the legislature held more power. Leading the Senate was Lieutenant Governor Bob Bullock—a Democrat; the Speaker of the House was Democrat Pete Laney.

George W. Bush called on both men and told them he wanted to work with them for the good of Texas. He arranged weekly breakfast meetings with them, and he began courting members of the State Legislature with his main theme of doing what was right for Texas. He excelled at the backroom meetings, one-on-one with legislators. He appointed Clay Johnson, his former college roommate, to recommend appointments to

Campaigning in New Orleans for the Democratic presidential ticket, former Texas Governor Ann Richards talks with reporters, October 31, 2000. Richards criticized Governor Bush's record and policy plans.

the various boards and commissions. He told Johnson to find the best people for the jobs and not let party politics enter into choices. A product of the good-old-boy system, George W. appointed some qualified people who had helped elect him, people who were loyal to him, people he could trust.

The Texas Legislature meets only 140 days in two years. When it was in session, George W. wheeled and dealed to make his campaign promises realities. And although legislation was passed on all four of his campaign issues, the bills did not encompass the issues. Plans were made to return control of education to local boards; several welfare cuts were passed; stricter penalties were set for juvenile offenders; and a bill was passed to reduce monetary rewards for frivolous lawsuits.

When the legislature wasn't in session, time weighed heavily on George W's hands. A *Texas Monthly* article lined out his working day as starting at the office at 8:00. He'd leave around 11:40 for a jog and lunch, and then return around 1:30. If there were no meetings, he stayed in his office to be available, but played video golf or solitaire until 3:00. Evenings ended early. Official dinners were over by 9:00.

Appointments were brief. At the end of the allotted meeting time, an aide would knock on the door to end the meeting. If he needed more time, George W. would wave the aide away, but he'd expect a second knock five minutes later. George W. relied on his staff to thoroughly research issues and present them to him in a summary, not a lengthy policy report. He'd read the summaries, and then hone in on crucial elements. He'd assign an aide an opposing view, so that he had both sides of issues.

Trusting the consensus opinions of his commissions, George W. usually reinforced their decisions. Most decisions were not headline makers, but two very different cases claimed the public's opinion. In both cases, the governor followed the same criteria in seconding the Texas Board of Pardons and Paroles' opinion, which was: "Is there any doubt about the guilt of the individual, and has the individual had a fair hearing and full access to the courts?"

The first case dealt with pickax murderer Karla Faye Tucker. In prison she became a born-again Christian, and the

Fllen Burns chants in protest of the death penalty at a rally held at the State Capitol in Austin, Texas on January 17, 1998, to prevent the execution of convicted murderer Karla Faye Tucker, planned for February 3.

evangelical community, along with celebrities and anti-capital punishment groups, asked that George W. step in and grant her a 30-day delay, all that a Texas governor is allowed for a death-row inmate, so she could seek further legal action, even though in this case there was no doubt that she was guilty. She did not pass George W.'s two-question test for clemency, so he allowed the execution of the first woman in Texas since the Civil War.

The second case involved Henry Lee Lucas, the self-proclaimed serial killer. He was convicted of killing a woman, identified as "Orange Socks" for the only clothing she was wearing when her body was found. He confessed to that killing and hundreds of others, but later he recanted the Orange Socks murder. Proof emerged after the trial that he was in Florida when the killing occurred. The prison board advised the governor to stop the execution. Again, George W. applied his two-question test. Lucas is the only death-row inmate whose execution was stopped, and in court he was sentenced to life in prison, with no possibility of parole.

His capital punishment decisions were brought up by George W.'s opponent, Garry Mauro, in the 1998 campaign for governor, but another issue received more press. Was George W. biding time in Texas awaiting a run for the country's top job? In Republican meetings, his name had surfaced countless times as a contender.

George W.'s standard reply to the questions was, "I don't know whether I'll seek the presidency or not." He stuck to Texas politics during the campaign and earned the backing of many Democrats in the legislature, including Senate leader Bob Bullock. It was no surprise when George W. Bush won with an impressive 67% of the vote, the first time a Texas governor had been elected to successive terms.

Still, The Question arose again and again. Some reports surfaced that a possible presidential bid looming in the distance prompted the partners in the Rangers to sell the team. George W. received around $15 million for his share. Now he was free to pursue a higher office without regard to his financial future if he weren't elected.

The morning of his second inaugural as governor, George W. listened to the minister speak at a special service. Pastor

Mark Craig said that people are "starved for leadership, starved for leaders who have ethical and moral courage." People wanted leaders who would do what was right.

"He was talking to you," Barbara Bush later told her eldest son.

George W. thought so, too, and set his sights on Washington.

Former President George H.W. Bush, left, shakes hands with his
son, Texas Governor George W. Bush, during a Republican rally held
in Houston on November 2, 1998.

8

A Contested Election

Before Reality Day for the elections of 1998, the elder George Bush wrote a letter to George W. and to Jeb, who was once again running for governor of Florida. He told them not to worry about what reporters wrote even though it could be hurtful to their family:

> At some point both of you may want to say "Well, I don't agree with my Dad on that point" or "Frankly I think Dad was wrong on that." Do it. Chart your own course, not just on the issues but on defining yourselves. No one will ever question your love of family—your devotion to your parents.

The brothers won the elections in their respective states, and for George W. the road that led to Washington was filled with the pitfalls of comparisons that his father had foreseen. The two shared the same name, except that George W. was missing the Herbert in his father's name, and the son strikingly resembled his father. Not since John Adams and John Quincy Adams had a son followed his father to the presidency, so the possibility of it happening again caused a media frenzy.

Once George W. decided to run, he knew he had home-work. His knowledge of foreign affairs was nil, so as was his custom, he surrounded himself with knowledgeable people, many of whom had worked for his father's administration, and listened to their different views on the United States' relations with various countries. He also needed to define his own issues, much as he had when he ran for governor.

The presidential race would be character-based. President Bill Clinton's dalliance with a White House intern and later impeachment, but not conviction on charges of obstruction of justice and perjury before a grand jury in a civil case, made voters think of who they wanted to lead the country in terms of trust. But before George W. could face the Clinton-tainted Democratic nominee, most likely vice president Al Gore (although he was challenged briefly by Former Senator Bill Bradley), George W. had to win the Republican nomination.

The field of Republican candidates widened as more and more candidates threw their hats in the ring. By September 1999, several candidates had dropped out, but eight remained. George W. was the front-runner, but Arizona senator John McCain was closing in. Others in the field included Gary Bauer, ultraconservative who had worked in the Reagan White House; Elizabeth Dole, former Secretary of Transportation and former Secretary of Labor; Steve Forbes, wealthy publishing giant; Orrin Hatch, senator from Utah; Alan Keyes, who previ-ously worked at the United Nations and the state department, but had never held elective office; and Dan Quayle, former vice president under George Bush.

Although in his earlier campaigns, George W. had not brought up his family connections, in the presidential campaign he did not discourage questions about his parents. When one reporter asked why he was the frontrunner, he quipped, "Maybe it's because I have a famous mother." Name recognition, critical to candidates, was not a problem for him.

"His personality and temperament come from Barbara," said his wife, Laura. "They both love to needle and they both love to talk." Bush even wisecracked that he had his father's eyes and his mother's mouth, not a bad comment considering that Barbara Bush is one of America's most admired first ladies.

George W. had become a strong campaigner. *Texas Monthly* writer Paul Burka noted his style when he followed the governor during a 1998 campaign trip, a style George W. continued during the presidential bid.

> He works a crowd the old fashioned way, going through it rather than waiting for the people to come to him. He makes eye contact and holds it; I followed him around the room in Eastland [Texas] and I never once saw his eyes stray from a voter to survey the room. Bush is a toucher: he doesn't shake a hand so much as grab it; he leans in close, clutches an arm, pats a shoulder, gives a hug. "Hey, buddy," he'll say, or "'Preciate your takin' the time."

The governor's campaign style stood him in good stead as he moved toward the primaries in 2000, but once again questions of his youthful behavior surfaced. Responding to reporters' questions on purported drug use, he answered maybe he did or maybe he didn't. He maintained that questions about past behavior were not relevant to the election.

He said, "When I was young and irresponsible, I was young and irresponsible," and he refused to elaborate. He wanted the election to be about the issues and who a person was as an adult.

Although John McCain posed a serious threat in the first of the primaries, by Super Tuesday in March, when fourteen states elected delegates to the Republican National Convention, George W. was all but guaranteed the nomination. Through the

Republican presidential hopeful George W. Bush hugs one of a crowd of students who greeted him upon his arrival at Bennett-Kew Elementary School in Inglewood, California on September 2, 1999. The visit, where he decried federal education policies that "cheat poor children," was a forum for Bush to lay out his first education proposals of the 2000 campaign.

remaining primaries, he campaigned not against other Republicans, but aimed his rhetoric at Al Gore, who also had virtually won the Democratic nomination when the votes were counted on Super Tuesday. The vice president had been in national politics for more than two decades. George W. was a novice on the national level. Instead of decrying the difference, he played up the outsider role, claiming he would bring fresh ideas to Washington.

At the Republican National Convention, George W. Bush was selected as the party's candidate. George W. asked Dick Cheney, former congressman from Wyoming and Secretary of

Defense in George Bush's administration, to be his running mate and campaign for the vice presidency.

At the Democratic National Convention, Al Gore picked Joe Lieberman, senator from Connecticut, as his running mate. Other candidates represented small political parties, most notably environmentalist Ralph Nader, running for president for the Green Party, and ultraconservative Pat Buchanan, the presidential candidate for the Reform Party.

After the conventions and until Reality Day on November 7, the candidates campaigned fast and furious. George W.'s campaign, under the direction of Don Evans, set records for fundraising. The Republicans were ready to stand behind a man who said he was a compassionate conservative who could serve both the right wing conservatives of the party and the more moderate Republicans. The campaign chest held more than $90 million, and George W. refused matching funds from the government that came with strings attached. His campaign could spend campaign money without government regulations.

George W. came across to campaign crowds as friendlier than Al Gore, who seemed stiff and formal. On national TV and radio, George W. faced Al Gore in three debates. Both sides claimed victories, although Al Gore earned criticism for his loud sighs, interrupting, and arrogant behavior. "Arrogant" had been a word applied to George W. during his youth, but he had learned to stay cool, calm, and conveyed a confident air at the debates. Polls of viewers showed that the debates did not change the mind of voters who had already settled on one candidate.

On the Thursday before the Tuesday election, reports circulated that 24 years earlier Bush had been convicted of driving while under the influence of alcohol. Bush admitted that was true but said he had changed. The Bush camp hoped the news would not influence the evangelical right to vote against him and flashed back to the university beer bash ad during that long ago congressional election in Texas.

ELECTION CONTROVERSY

On November 7, the presidential race was too close to call. Polls by both parties showed that some states would go strongly for Al Gore and others would easily elect George W. Bush, but there were a handful of states in which the candidates were evenly matched. In each state, the candidates were competing for the popular vote, which would dictate which way the electors in the Electoral College would cast their votes.

Instead of electing the president and vice president by popular vote, each state has electors, the same number as the state has U.S. Congressmen (decided by the state's population) and senators (two). Of the 538 electoral votes, a candidate needed 270 to win the presidency. The Electoral College was included in the Constitution to balance large and small states. If it did not exist, states with large populations, such as New York, Texas, and California, could control an election, and the election would not be a true national contest.

Both candidates settled in for the long wait. With the election so close, it could be well into the night before a president was elected. In Austin, George W. gathered his friends and family around him. Jeb was with him that evening, as were the 41st president and Barbara Bush.

The Bush family was dining at a restaurant when television newscasters called Florida for Al Gore. Florida was an important state, with 25 electoral votes. Jeb didn't believe the call; he was convinced that George W. would win that state. The family retreated to the privacy of the governor's mansion where they could view the results, which at that moment did not look promising.

The Voter News Service, headquartered that night in the World Trade Center, is jointly owned by television networks (CBS, ABC, NBC, Fox, CNN) and the Associated Press. On Election Day, thousands of temporary employees stood outside voting places and conducted exit polls. They recorded age, race, gender, religion, income, past voting tendencies and who a

Republican presidential candidate Texas Governor George W. Bush, right, and Democratic presidential candidate Vice President Al Gore debate on October 3, 2000 at the Clark Athletic Center on the campus of the University of Massachusetts in Boston.

person voted for. This information was sent to computer banks at VNS that plugged the numbers into statistical models and forecasted the winner of each state. In many states a winner could have been announced by early afternoon, but networks waited until polls closed in a state before predicting the winner. But on November 7, newscasters called Florida before the polls closed in the panhandle, which is in the Central time zone.

Jeb Bush phoned campaign workers in Florida and discovered that something wasn't right. The samplings VNS based their call on were distorted toward Gore. The Bush camp was cheered by the news, but the networks stood by their call. Team Bush was concerned that the call, which made it look like Gore would win the presidency, could influence voters not to vote in a losing cause in other states, where polls were open for two more hours.

Quickly two other key states, Pennsylvania and Michigan, were tallied in the Gore column, and the Bush camp was somber until the central border states (Missouri; Tennessee, Al Gore's home state; Arkansas, Clinton's home state) were called for Bush. It was not until shortly after 10:00 P.M. that the networks recalled Florida and placed it in the too-close-to-call category. A couple hours later, with the reported electoral count at 246 for Bush and 255 for Gore, it was clear that those 25 electoral votes in Florida would determine the presidency. Around two in the morning, Florida was called for George W. Bush with a 50,000-vote lead, and the networks named him the next president. Al Gore called George W. and conceded. Gore left his hotel suite to deliver his concession speech at his headquarters. Before he reached the podium, his advisors had learned that the margin in Florida was a mistake, a computer glitch, and only several hundred votes separated the two candidates, which meant an automatic machine recount of votes, mandated by Florida state law. Gore called George W. and retracted his concession, saying that Florida was still too close to call.

By daylight Wednesday, George W. Bush led the tally by less than 2,000 votes. A machine recount began immediately. Lawyers from both sides descended on Florida. On Thursday the Gore Team asked for hand recounts in four heavily Democratic counties. In every election in every state, votes are not counted because of voter error, but the percentage was unusually high in some Florida counties. Here punch-type ballots were used, and if a chad, a rectangle that was to be punched out, wasn't fully disconnected, the machine would not count it. These were "undervotes," and the Democrats wanted every one counted where the voter's intent could be determined.

By Friday the machine recount was finished. Gore trailed by barely 300 votes (without absentee ballots counted), and his team was adamant that the undervotes be counted. A few

Bush, flanked by his father and one of his brothers, Florida Governor Jeb Bush, watches election returns in Austin on November 7, 2000. Fickle voting machines produced a deadlock with the highest possible stakes for the nation. One year later, the terrorist attacks of September 11 handed to President Bush a mandate the likes of which have not been seen since World War II.

precincts using punch-type ballots were counted on a trial basis, but the standard of perceiving voter intent was controversial. If a chad hung by two sides, was it a vote? Or if the chad was punctured, but didn't dislodge any sides—was that a vote? What about a "dimpled" chad? Perhaps the voter meant to vote, but didn't push hard enough with the stylus. The Gore camp would benefit if every dimpled chad were counted. The Bush camp protested.

The Democrats also cried foul over a butterfly ballot used in one county that listed the ten slates of president/vice president candidates from large and small political parties on both sides of the ballot with the voting holes in the middle. This ballot

President-elect Bush and his wife, Laura, acknowledge applause after his address to the nation from the chamber of the Texas House of Representatives in Austin on December 13, 2000.

confused some voters, who voted for more than one candidate for president.

Many lawsuits were filed in both state and federal courts asking to hand count the ballots, stop the hand count, extend the deadline for counting, stay the extension, challenge the overseas ballots, challenge the standard of counting, etc. Late evening on December 12, in a five to four decision, the U.S. Supreme Court decided that the deadline would not allow a recount that had no fair and uniform standard. Many Democrats felt they had been cheated out of a victory; many Republicans felt the election was finally legitimate.

On December 13, Al Gore gave a gracious concession speech on national television. He said it was time to put partisan rancor aside. Although he disagreed with the Supreme

Court ruling, he said he accepted it. "[T]onight," he said, "for the sake of our unity of the people and the strength of our democracy, I offer my concession."

George W. Bush gave his victory speech in the chamber of the Texas House of Representatives. He mentioned that he understood how difficult this was for the vice president, then moved on to speak in reconciliatory terms.

> I was not elected to serve one party, but to serve one nation. The president of the United States is the president of every single American, of every race and every background. Whether you voted for me or not, I will do my best to serve your interests, and I will work to earn your respect.

The controversial election with Supreme Court intervention caused concern and dismay across America. After George W. Bush was declared the winner, several news organizations began independent examination of the undervote and overvote. In June 2001, *USA Today* and several other newspapers declared Bush won the election by using three of four standards of evaluating undervote ballots. However, if the overvote was counted, those ballots that had more than one vote for president, Gore's name was punched in combination with others more often than Bush's. It would be hard to discern voter intent from these ballots. Some people had voted for all ten candidates.

One thing was clear. Election equipment and voter education needed to be addressed, not only in Florida, but across the nation.

George W. Bush takes the oath of office from U.S. Supreme Court Chief Justice William Rehnquist to become the 43d president, Saturday, January 20, 2001, in Washington.

9

Leading
the Nation

On January 20, 2001, George Walker Bush became the 43rd president in an inaugural ceremony in Washington, D.C. Instead of immediately focusing on him, media followed the news story of former president Bill Clinton because of his questionable eleventh hour pardons of many people. This time without a great deal of media hype allowed President Bush to settle into Washington life surrounded by people he trusted in their loyalty to him and in their expertise in their fields. His appointees to the Cabinet were made and confirmed by the Senate.

The president was well versed in domestic issues, but was quickly forced to focus on foreign policy. In February, U.S. submarine *Greeneville* surfaced in a routine drill and hit a Japanese fishing boat, killing nine people on board and injuring others. The situation called for delicate handling, and President Bush informed the Japanese that he "regretted" the incident and promised an investigation.

In March, disturbing news from Afghanistan reached the America art world. The Taliban, the radical Muslim rulers of that country, declared that two huge Buddha statues, both between 1,800 and 1,600 years old, were blasphemous and must be destroyed. Although other nations, including the United States, viewed the statues as artistic treasures, the Taliban destroyed them.

In April, an American spy plane made an emergency landing on a Chinese island after colliding with a Chinese plane. The Chinese demanded an apology, and they would not release either the 24-member crew or the plane. Days later, the president again used the word *regret* to show remorse on the part of the Americans for violating Chinese airspace. The men were returned and the plane was shipped in pieces back to the United States. It appeared that U.S-Chinese relations were not harmed because of this situation.

In May, national affairs demanded the attention of the Bush White House. The FBI discovered it had not turned over some 3,000 documents to the defense team of terrorist Timothy McVeigh, convicted of the 1995 bombing of the federal building in Oklahoma City that killed 168 people. The Justice Department delayed McVeigh's scheduled May 16 execution until attorneys could determine if the additional documents could have changed the defense. The outcome only delayed McVeigh's execution until June 11, but questions were raised about the death penalty, which President Bush had dealt with head-on when he was governor of Texas.

Also on the domestic scene, President Bush faced a challenge to his legislative agenda by the party switch of Vermont senator James Jeffords from Republican to Independent. The change gave control of the Senate to the Democrats and caused a realignment of majority and minority leadership in the Senate.

In New York City, two Muslim extremists were convicted of

the 1998 bombings of United States embassies in Kenya and Tanzania where 224 people were killed. The two were linked to the international terrorist organization al-Queda, lead by Osama bin Laden, who had made clear he did not want American presence in the Holy Land. Among the documents entered into testimony was a training manual that directed terrorists to blend into the country where they were sent. The terrorist threat was seen to be overseas.

By August, President Bush announced his decision on federal funds used for stem cell research. A scientific advance showed that embryonic stem cells could regenerate tissue for many parts of the body. Anti-abortion groups opposed the use of embryonic stem cells, calling them part of a human being, even though many of the stem cells were from in-vitro storage and would be thrown away. President Bush presented a compromise. He allowed federal funds for research on the 64 lines already in development, but disallowed funding for new lines.

Then the September 11 terrorist attacks against the World Trade Center and the Pentagon changed the world. President Bush focused on getting aid to the victims and families and stopping terrorism.

He gathered his carefully chosen advisors around him on the morning of September 15 at Camp David, the presidential retreat in Maryland. He listened to Central Intelligence Agency Director George Tenet, who had been appointed by Clinton and retained by the new president because he thought the man was trustworthy and intelligent. Tenet outlined his plan for a war against the terrorist training camps headed by Osama bin Laden in Afghanistan: use both CIA officers and military commandos to aid Afghanistan's Northern Alliance, the anti-Taliban force, while airplanes dropped bombs on terrorist camps and Taliban strongholds. General Hugh Shelton, Chairman of the Joint Chiefs of Staff, presented four military options. Secretary of State Colin Powell said a coalition of

Exiled Saudi dissident Osama bin Laden is seen in this April 1998 photograph from Afghanistan. Bin Laden has been suspected of involvement in bombings of the U.S. embassies in Kenya and Tanzania in August of 1998. He has threatened a holy war against U.S. troops and Americans in general and may have been behind other terrorist attacks, including a 1996 attack on Saudi Arabia and, more recently, the September 11 attack.

Muslim nations supporting the U.S. war would crumble if the war were waged outside of Afghanistan. Secretary of Defense Donald Rumsfeld and National Security Adviser Condoleezza Rice agreed that necessary risk to operatives would be involved.

Shortly after lunch, Bush told his team of advisers to get some rest and exercise and report back at 4:00. At that meeting, he asked for individual votes. All voted for military action, but there were different votes on what type of action to take. He thanked them all and told them he needed time to think about it.

By the next afternoon at the White House, Bush had made a decision. He wanted the war marketed as a fight against terrorism, which threatened all nations, instead of merely an American retaliation. The campaign would start in Afghanistan with both CIA and military operatives.

President Bush met with Pakistani General Pervez Musharraf to discuss a military operations base in Pakistan. The president left the details to his staff, as was his custom. He decided broad policy and expected his staff to implement his decisions.

On October 7, he addressed the American people on national television from the Treaty Room in the White House, announcing he had ordered air strikes to commence in Afghanistan in an operation called Enduring Freedom. To show the Afghan people that the war was against terrorists, not them, he also announced the dropping of food and medical supplies.

> We are joined in this operation by our staunch friend, Great Britain. Other close friends, including Canada, Australia, Germany and France, have pledged forces as the operation unfolds. More than forty countries in the Middle East, Africa, Europe and across Asia have granted air transit or landing rights. Many more have shared intelligence. We are supported by the collective will of the world.

He told Americans that the war would require patience and sacrifice. He warned that it would not be without risk of life, and he thanked the men and women of the military who would be fighting the war on foreign soil. "Your mission is defined; your objectives are clear; your goal is just. You have my full confidence, and you will have every tool you need to carry out your duty."

When a few weeks later the campaign seemed stalled and the press emphasized that the war was bogging down, President Bush did not lose faith. At a meeting with his advisors, he stopped their voiced concerns about the war. "We did all agree on the plan, didn't we?" They agreed. "I've made it clear to the American people. I've got confidence in this plan. We should all have confidence in this plan. Be patient, people. It's going to work."

A few days later, the Taliban retreated from several cities, and the fall of the zealots looked imminent. President Bush was pleased, but he knew the war against worldwide terrorism was not over. And bin Laden's location was unknown.

At home, another element of terrorism further threatened previously complacent Americans. Anthrax, a deadly bacterium, had been sent in letters to a television newscaster and to a senator and a congressman. Post offices were scrutinized. A government office building was shut down while it was sanitized. Security measures were implemented for those handling mail. Tom Ridge, director of the newly created agency Homeland Security, handled the security details, while FBI agents followed every lead in an effort to find the person responsible for several anthrax deaths.

The economy, which had been falling, continued a slide into a recession despite interest rate cuts. In order to promote the economy, President Bush traveled through the Midwest following the route of products from the time they were manufactured to their export and advocated increasing the selling of agricultural products abroad.

As President Bush moved into his second year as the chief executive, he faced world and domestic problems head-on and informed Americans that solutions would not be easy. He

Plumes of smoke rise from the Taliban-controlled village of Rahesh on the Shomali plain, north of Afghanistan's capital Kabul on November 9, 2001, after two U.S. air strikes. Punishing American air strikes on Taliban positions north of the capital helped the forces of the Northern Alliance to break through outer Taliban defenses. In 10 tumultuous days, the Taliban lost two thirds of its territory and saw many of the trappings of its government fall into the hands of its greatest enemies.

Bush speaks in Knoxville, Tennessee, on April 8, 2002. Bush praised local officials who have coordinated the Citizen Corps that Bush called for in his State of the Union address and spoke of the continuing need for citizens to volunteer their time.

reminded Americans that the war in Afghanistan would not be over until that nation had a stable government. The hunt for terrorists in other countries would continue through a combined effort of nations.

President Bush had been elected during peacetime, but events thrust him into global leadership as the world took on international terrorism. He believed that the job was his calling, and his leadership qualities were equal to the tasks ahead.

1946 Born George Walker Bush on July 6 in New Haven, Connecticut

1948 Moves with family to Texas

1961 Enters Phillips Academy in Andover, Massachusetts

1964 Works as a campaign aide for his father's senate race; enters Yale University

1968 Graduates from Yale; joins Texas Air National Guard

1973 Enters Harvard Business School

1975 Graduates from Harvard Business School; moves to Midland, Texas, to work in the oil industry

1977 Decides to run for U.S. Congress; meets Laura Welch in the summer and marries her on November 5; forms Arbusto oil company

1978 Wins Republican primary for congressman in June; loses general election in November

1981 George W. Bush's father becomes vice president of the United States; Laura gives birth to twin daughters, Jenna Welch Bush and Barbara Pierce Bush on November 25

1984 Merges his oil company with Spectrum 7

1986 Sells Spectrum 7 to Harken Energy, which retains him as a director

1987 Moves to Washington, D.C., to help with his father's presidential campaign

1988 His father is elected president of the United States; at the end of the year, George W. moves his family to Dallas

1989 Helps put together a group of investors to buy the Texas Rangers baseball team; becomes managing general partner and deals with the public and press

1990 Sells Harken Energy stock to pay off his debt for Texas Rangers

1994 Runs for governor and defeats incumbent Ann Richards

1998   Sells interest in Texas Rangers; Wins a second consecutive term as governor

1999   Enters presidential race

2000   Wins contested presidential race against Al Gore

2001   **January** Inaugurated as the 43rd president of the United States
April Confrontation with China over detention of a U.S. spy plane and its 24 crewmen

June Bush signs a tax cut legislation into law. Refund checks begin to flow in late summer.

September 11 Attacks on the World Trade Center and the Pentagon, executed by al-Qaeda under the direction of Osama bin Laden, catapult the United States into the War on Terror.

October American troops go into Afghanistan to rout the Taliban who gave safe harbor to the al-Qaeda terrorists involved in 9/11.

2002   **January** President Bush's State of the Union address identifies Iraq, North Korea, and Iran as the "Axis of evil" and makes them potential targets of the War on Terror.
February The United States rejects the Kyoto Treaty, an environmental protocol intended to cut down on worldwide emissions, stem global warming, and benefit environmental quality.

June Bush proposes the Department of Homeland Security to better coordinate the agencies responsible for securing our nation. Tom Ridge becomes the administration's first Homeland Security Advisor.

November The Republican Party takes over both houses of the Congress, which is expected to give Bush a mandate for his programs.

2003   **January** The Homeland Security Act takes effect.
January President Bush devotes much of his State of the Union address to outlining the justifications for invading Iraq to overthrow Saddam Hussein.

March 19 At 9:34 P.M. EST the second Persian Gulf War begins.

Bush, George with Victor Gold. *Looking Forward: An Autobiography.* Garden City, New York: Doubleday, 1987.

Dershowitz, Alan M. *Supreme Injustice: How the High Court Hijacked Election 2000.* New York: Oxford University Press, 2001.

Greenfield, Jeff. *"Oh, Waiter! One Order of Crow!"* New York: G.P. Putnam's Sons, 2001.

Lewis, Charles and the Center for Public Integrity. *The Buying of the President, 2000.* New York: Avon, 2000.

Mitchell, Elizabeth. *W: Revenge of the Bush Dynasty.* NY: Hyperion, 2000.

Political Staff of *The Washington Post. Deadlock: The Inside Story of America's Closest Election.* New York: Public Affairs, 2001.

Radcliffe, Donnie. *Simply Barbara Bush: A Portrait of America's Candid First Lady.* New York: Warner, 1989.

Bush, Barbara. *A Memoir*. NY: Charles Scribner's Sons, 1994.

Bush, George. *All the Best: My Life in Letters and Other Writings*. New York: Scribner, 1999.

Bush, George W. *A Charge to Keep: My Journey to the White House*. New York: HarperCollins, 1999.

Gormley, Beatrice. *President George W. Bush: Our Forty-third President*. New York: Aladdin Paperbacks, 2001.

Greene, John Robert. *The Presidency of George Bush*. Lawrence, Kansas: University Press of Kansas, 2000.

Ivins, Molly and Dubose, Lou. *Shrub: The Short But Happy Political Life of George W. Bush*. New York: Random House, 2000.

Minutaglio, Bill. *First Son: George W. Bush and the Bush Family Dynasty*. New York: Random House, 1999.

Wukovits, John F. *George W. Bush*. San Diego: Lucent, 2000.

PICTURE CREDITS

VEDA BOYD JONES enjoys the challenge of writing for diverse readers. She is the author of 28 books, including fiction and nonfiction for both adults and children, and over 200 articles and stories for magazines and reference books. Jones earned a master's degree in history at the University of Arkansas; has taught writing at Crowder College in Neosho, Missouri; and teaches for the Institute of Children's Literature. She is currently president of the Missouri Writers' Guild. She and her husband, Jimmie, an architect, have three sons.

ARTHUR M. SCHLESINGER, jr. is the leading American historian of our time. He won the Pulitzer Prize for his book *The Age of Jackson* (1945) and again for a chronicle of the Kennedy Administration, *A Thousand Days* (1965), which also won the National Book Award. Professor Schlesinger is the Albert Schweitzer Professor of the Humanities at the City University of New York and has been involved in several other Chelsea House projects, including the series REVOLUTIONARY WAR LEADERS, COLONIAL LEADERS, and YOUR GOVERNMENT.

04   06